GW01081090

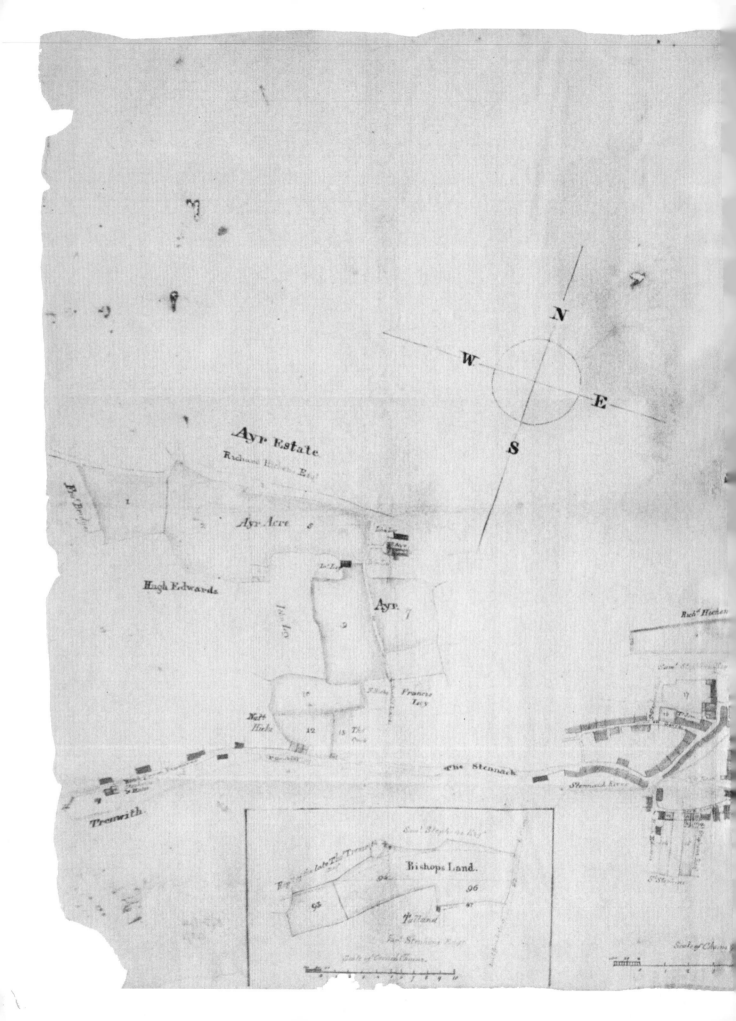

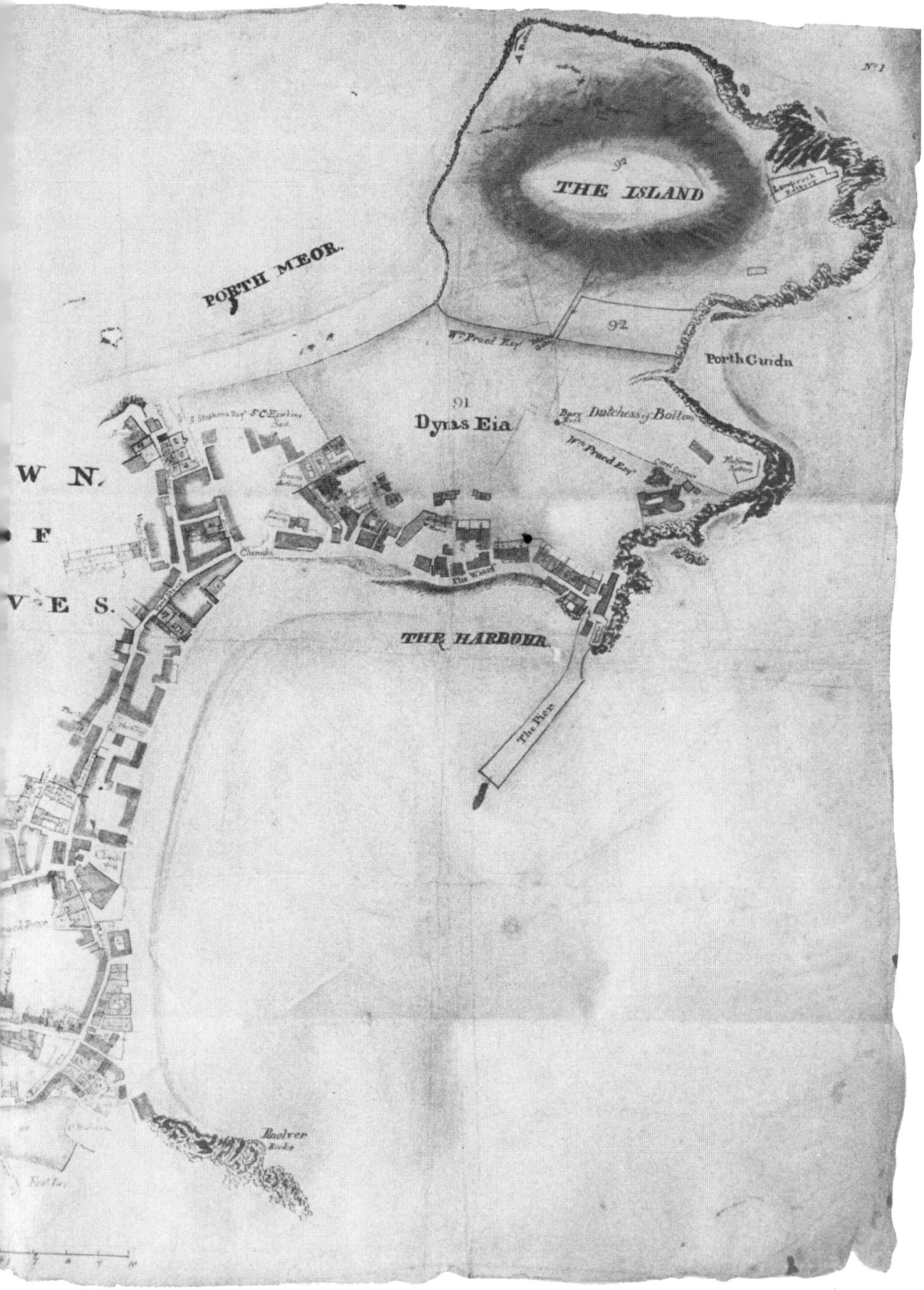

THE ISLAND

PORTH MEOR.

Wᵐ Proed Esq

92

Porth Cuidn

91

Dynas Eia

S Stephens Esq Sᵗ C Hawkins Bart

Bury Dutchess of Bolton Esq

Wᵐ Proed Esq

TOWN. OF IVES.

Church

THE HARBOUR.

The Wharf

The Pier

Paolver Rocks

THE BOOK OF ST IVES

FRONT COVER: St Ives, c1850, drawn and engraved by W. Willis of Penzance.

The lasting appeal of St Ives—a study of Carnglaze, c1900. (SSI)

THE BOOK OF ST IVES

A HISTORY OF THE TOWN

BY

CYRIL NOALL

BARON
BUCKINGHAM
MMXI

Also by Cyril Noall

Beloved St Ives (1958)
Cornish Midsummer Eve bonfire celebrations (1963)
Wreck & Rescue [three vols] (1964/5)
History of Cornish Mail & Stage Coaches (1968)
Penzance Library (1968)
St Ives Museum (1968)
Cornish Lights & Shipwrecks (1968)
Cornish Shipwrecks (1969)
The Story of St Ives (1970)
The Story of Cornwall's Lifeboats (1970)
The Story of Cornwall's Ports & Harbours (1970)
Levant: the Mine Beneath the Sea (1970)
Tales of Cornish Fishermen (1970)
Smuggling in Cornwall (1971)
Botallack (1972)
Cornish Seines and Seiners (1972)
St Just Mining District (1973)
St Ives Museum Guide (1977)
The Illustrated Past: Penwith (1978)
Harveys (1979)
Yesterday's Town: St Ives (1979)
St Ives Mining District (1982)
Geevor Tin Mines (1983)
The Book of Penzance (1983)
The Book of Hayle (1984)

Originally published in 1977
Second edition 1984
Third impression 2000
Fourth edition 2011

PUBLISHED BY BARON BOOKS OF BUCKINGHAM
IN THIS FOURTH EDITION IN 2011
AND PRODUCED BY CPI ANTONY ROWE

© Executor of the late Cyril Noall

ISBN 978 0 9566287 1 8

All rights reserved. No part of this publication may be reproduced, stored in a retrieval system, or transmitted, in any form or by any means, electronic, mechanical, photocopying, recording or otherwise, without the prior permission of Baron Books.

Any copy of this book issued by the Publishers as clothbound or as paperback is sold subject to the condition that it shall not by way of trade or otherwise, be lent, re-sold, hired out or otherwise circulated without the Publisher's prior consent, in any form of binding or cover other than that in which it is published, and without a similar condition including this condition being imposed on a subsequent publisher.

Contents

The Book of St Ives
in this fourth edition
is dedicated
to the memory of

CYRIL NOALL
a proper Cornishman,
a gentle man and
a true son of St Ives

Foreword

by Brian Stevens, Hon Curator, St Ives Museum and Recorder for St Ives, Old Cornwall Society

As it is now thirty-four years since Cyril Noall's *The Book of St Ives* was first published in 1977 and, with a second 1984 edition and a third 2000 impression produced since then, it seems most appropriate in 2011 that another edition is being made available to a new generation of St Ives folk. Cyril, who died in 1984 was, to those many who knew him, a worthy son of our town for, the pen being mightier than the sword, he ensured that we retain many and varied aspects of the history of this place.

Combined in this one book are the results of over twenty years of diligent research, certified by the hundreds of articles he wrote for our local paper, county newspapers, and magazines. Those reading this book must ultimately acknowledge the invaluable legacy that Cyril has bequeathed.

Monetary wealth was never his to seek or gain but, of far greater value, Cyril was respected for his approach, not only to the objects of his research, but the grace and humility with which he expressed himself to those who helped him. This was proved by his seemingly ever-ongoing task of gathering the fragments of our town's past, so that nothing may be lost by future generations, and so that we and others might glean and expand our knowledge, through his relentless delving back in time.

Cyril Noall's writings over some 55 years have been read by many. Now those who are privileged to obtain a copy of this new edition have the opportunity to share his beloved St Ives by way of words and illustrations. Do likewise, and you will not be disappointed.

Brian Stevens.

Foreword

by the Rev D. C. Freeman

When John Hobson Matthews prefaced his 'History of St Ives' in 1891 with the words 'The author is happy to believe that he has, at all events, served in some small degree the cause of historical truth,' he would have found it hard to believe that another eighty-six years would elapse before a worthy successor to his efforts could be found. Those who read this book will have no doubt that Cyril Noall has served well the cause of historical truth and given to another generation a fascinating glimpse of that which makes St Ives not simply a beautiful town but also a delightful community of which one is proud to be a member.

That community is already deeply indebted to Cyril Noall for his work on the history of St Ives, and this more extensive study will bring great joy to thousands throughout the world who know and love both town and people.

THE VICARAGE,
ST ANDREWS STREET

Douglas Freeman

Preface

by Alan Harvey, Mayor of St Ives

To anyone but Cyril Noall, the thought of the research necessary to write a book about St Ives would be a daunting task, but Cyril seems to have tireless energy when delving into the history of Cornwall and especially St Ives.

Many is the time I have seen him from my home going up the Stennack, and into the moorlands of Towednack, Zennor and Halsetown; these are walks that to most of us are enjoyable, but to Cyril Noall with all his knowledge, they are truly walks into the past. Does he, I wonder, as he strolls through Halsetown, actually see the tin miners starting their journey to their hard, dangerous work in the bowels of the earth? Or as he walks along the sea front to his beloved museum does he hear again the cry of 'Hevva! Hevva!' as the fishermen race out to net the shoal of pilchards?

It is fitting that this book should be published in 1977, as this year marks the centenary of the coming of the railway to St Ives. For, truly, that opened up St Ives to the world, and the world to St Ives; it also enabled the mackerel and herring then caught here in such vast quantities to be forwarded to distant markets in perfect condition. People from the four corners of the world were able to travel along the branch line from St Erth to St Ives; and who can make that trip, without marvelling not only at the engineering skill of its builders, but also at the amount of care that was taken not to destroy any of the natural scenic beauty? And we talk today of conservationists!

ST IVES, 1977

Alan Harvey

Acknowledgements

I first wish to express my appreciation to William Thomas for the skill, patience and enthusiasm he has cheerfully shown in taking, copying and printing so many of the photographs used in this book. No effort has been too great, no problem too difficult for him, and the results of his diligence are everywhere apparent.

My thanks are also due to the following individuals and institutions for their help and co-operation: the ex-Mayor of St Ives, Mr Dorvil Jones, and the St Ives Town Council for permission to photograph the civic regalia and old Borough records, also their former and present Clerks, Tom Prideaux and Mr A. Ruberry; the Trustees of St Ives Museum for permission to photograph pictures and exhibits and for their support; the County Museum, Truro, for photographs and prints, with special thanks to H. L. Douch (Curator) and R. D. Penhallurick (Assistant Curator); P. L. Hull, County Archivist, and J. C. Edwards, of the County Record Office, Truro, for copies of documents and plans; Studio St Ives, Ltd, for photographs from their magnificent collection of historic local views; the late R. Hale, and John Farmer, past and present Cornwall County Librarians, for their support and interest, also the staff at St Ives branch library for their assistance; the Committee of the Penzance (Morrab Gardens) Library, and Mrs S. Balson, Librarian, for their co-operation and the use of Christopher Borlase's drawing of St Ives; P. A. S. Pool, of Penzance, for permission to quote from his transcript of the Penheleg MS; the Rev D. C. Freeman, Vicar of St Ives, Canon J. B. D. Cotter, Vicar of Towednack and Zennor, and the Rev G. B. Whittaker, Vicar of Lelant, for permission to photograph their respective churches; Canon A. S. Roberts, Vicar of St Anta and All Saints, Carbis Bay, for information regarding his church; the Rev Austin W. Delaney, OSB, Bognor Regis, for historical notes on St Ives Catholic Church; J. Vaughan, of the Map Library, British Library, for a copy of the first ed. 25 in. Ordnance Survey of St Ives; N. G. Cox, of the Public Record Office, for a reproduction of the 1296 Lelant Charter; Harold Franklin, for the use of his fine collection of Edward Ashton negatives; S. Bennetts, E. T. Berryman and Percy Quick, for photographs; John T. Barber, for permission to quote 'Doble's Wall'.

Finally, a tribute must be paid to those early photographers, known and unknown, who, wrestling with heavy, primitive equipment, succeeded in producing pictures of high merit, many of them being genuine artistic creations.

The earliest dated photograph of St Ives—that of the New Pier stone-laying ceremony—was taken by James Moody of Penzance and Redruth in 1864. A little later came the Prestons of Penzance, who preserved delightful glimpses of the old George and Dragon and Golden Lion inns in the Market Place and other quaint buildings and corners long since swept away.

Mr Edward Ashton, a native of Plymouth, came to St Ives in 1866, where he opened a chemist's shop. For many years, particularly between 1870 and 1910, he faithfully recorded with his camera the town's changing aspect, amassing a huge collection of glass negatives which formed a wonderful historic record. Unfortunately, these have now been dispersed.

Mr W. Trevorrow is best known for his dramatic photographs of the great flood in 1894. With the enterprise of a modern press photographer, he captured many vivid scenes of the water rushing like a mighty river through the familiar streets and the general ruin to be seen afterwards. Mr J. C. Douglas, on the other hand, specialised in carefully composed

9

studies of the harbour and fishing fleet, some of his subjects in sepia bromide being awarded prizes in open competition and attracting world-wide notice. He was one of the senior members of the local art colony, and during his later years concentrated on painting in oils, achieving equally happy results in this medium. Mr Douglas died in 1938, having resided at St Ives for over half-a-century.

Mr L. E. Comley took many fine views of the town around the turn of the century; his unique pictures of 'huers' in action at the Baulking House and 'blowers' working on the capstans during a 'hevva' are in themselves sufficient to earn our grateful remembrance.

Mr W. J. Cooper combined the pursuits of photography and taxidermy; whilst Mr Herbert Lanyon photographed many delightful scenes in a St Ives that was still largely unspoilt by 'progress.'

Doble's Wall

There are those who once were young and strong,
    Now aged, bent and grey,
Who did the same in days of yore
    As youngsters do today.
Idly sitting in the sunshine,
    Lads together—big and small,
Such has always been the case
    On Doble's Wall.

Doble's Wall, Doble's Wall,
    There's 'no spot in all the world
Like Doble's Wall.

There are those in foreign lands today
    Who once were with us here;
Who wander back in memory
    To scenes they hold so dear;
But some day we hope to meet them,
    Meet together—one and all,
As we did in days gone by
    On Doble's Wall.

There are those who once were in our midst,
    Who'll ne'er again repeat
The summer songs we used to sing
    In harmony so sweet;
But their names we often mention
    As the twilight shadows fall,
And we gather as of old
    On Doble's Wall.

                                            John T. Barber

The Spirit of St Ives

Every town, irrespective of size or significance, possesses its own special attraction for those who call it home; but in the case of St Ives, that appeal, that tug at the heartstrings, has a truly magnetic power, drawing the exile back again and again to renew fond memories or revive old dreams, and making the stay-at-home everlastingly thankful that he has not to suffer the wrench of parting.

Of what ingredients is this magical, this irresistible charm of St Ives compounded? Some are immediately obvious to the most casual observer. The curving blue bay fringed by golden sands, the picturesque harbour with its kaleidoscopic range of activities, the fascinating maze of crooked, cobbled streets in the old fishing quarter, the delights of a legend-haunted countryside dotted with hill forts, menhirs, cromlechs and ruins of ancient mines, encompassing superlative moorland and cliff scenery—these are the attractions which during the past hundred years have made St Ives the Mecca of holidaymakers visiting West Cornwall.

But there are other qualities, more subtle, secret and elusive which bind the true St Ivesian to his native place with ties just as strong and sure—qualities scarcely even suspected by the tourists who choke its streets and throng its beaches every summer. These derive from the unique shared community experience of a people who for generations wrested a precarious livelihood from the sea, which welded them together into one large family whose members were ever ready to help one another in times of hardship and danger.

Sadly, the old fishing days which gave rise to these feelings of warm-hearted good neighbourliness have now departed, and their aftermath has brought about many changes in the old town. Some of these were necessary and beneficial, others needless and regretted by all. Happily, however, much of the essential St Ives remains unaltered, and the noble tower of the parish church still presides over a town on which Time has laid his hand more lightly than most.

In these pages an attempt has been made to reflect something of the true spirit of St Ives and its people, to chronicle its history from earliest times down to the present day, to describe its ancient customs and industries, and to give some account of its leading personalities and their influence on local affairs; above all, to portray, through the medium of old photographs, nostalgic scenes and happenings of the past with a fidelity and lack of bias impossible with the written word. Inevitably, the story, the picture, is incomplete; but if the living essence of the place is captured here, then this book has not altogether been written in vain.

St Ives, May 27, 1977.

Title page of the first volume of the Borough Accounts, 1570. (TC; WT)

St Ia's Cove

Though situated on the bleak, gale-lashed northern coast of Cornwall less than twenty miles from Land's End, St Ives occupies a relatively sheltered position at the north-west extremity of a sand-fringed bay, shielded from the prevailing winds by its bold headland, or Island, and the hills of the Penwith peninsula. To this favourable circumstance the place owed its rise as a fishing centre and seaport in late mediaeval times.

Of the prehistory of St Ives little is known, nearly all traces of early occupation having been obliterated by later development. A stone battle-axe was once found in the town; at both Chyangweal, and Hellesvean underground passages, or fogous, are known to have existed; at Carnellis and near Clodgy there are still to be seen primitive buildings conjecturally identified as 'Picts' houses.' The Island is thought to have been once a cliff castle, with a now vanished ditch and rampart across the sandy isthmus to secure it from landward attack; its old Cornish names of 'Pendinas' (fortified headland) and 'Dynas Ia' (Ia's fortress) certainly lend support to this idea.

The district around St Ives is, however, fairly rich in archaeological evidence. Outstanding among these is the massive cromlech at Zennor which, though capsized in a frolic by high-spirited young men from the neighbouring parish of Towednack during the early 19th century and further mutilated in 1861 by Henry Grenfell, a farmer (who wished to convert it into a cattle shed) is one of the most impressive Cornish monuments to early man.

Flat-topped Trencrom Hill to the south of St Ives is capped by an ancient fortress with great stone ramparts and gateways and numerous hut circles; fragments of Iron Age pottery have been found here, together with two Neolithic axes. Prior to its silting up in the 14th century, the deep and sheltered tidal estuary at Lelant, running in from the head of St Ives Bay, was a busy harbour where early traders between Ireland and the Continent landed their goods, carrying them the few miles overland to St Michael's Mount for reshipment to avoid the dangerous Land's End passage; the route was overlooked and guarded by the Trencrom hill fort.

Striking proof of this old trading link with Ireland came to light on December 11 1931, when E. T. Berryman discovered the now famous Bronze Age Towednack gold hoard at Amalveor, about three miles inland from St Ives. With other finds made on May 25 of the following year, this comprised a torc of twisted gold wire with another of unique treble form, three gold bracelets (one unfinished) and three bent bars of gold. They were dated at 1000-750 BC, being of Irish gold and workmanship; all are now in the British Museum.

St Ives enters recorded history with the arrival of St Ia, or Hya, the Irish princess who introduced Christianity to this district in the 5th century. The earliest account we possess of her is the *Vita Guigneri*, a life of St Gwinear, written about the year 1300 by one Anselm, a clerk. He describes how Gwinear and his fellow missionaries, when leaving Ireland for Cornwall, 'had not gone far, when a virgin of noble birth, named Hya, came down to the shore, meaning to go with them. Finding she was too late, she knelt down on the beach in great grief and prayed. As she did so, she noticed a little leaf floating on the water. She touched it with the rod she carried to see if it would sink, and lo! it began to grow bigger and bigger as she looked at it. She saw that it was sent to her by God, and, trusting to Him, she embarked upon the leaf, and was straightway wafted across the Channel, reaching her destination before the others.'

William of Worcester, writing in 1478, adds a little more to the story. He describes her as 'Saint Hya, that is Seynt Hy, the sister of St Herygh (Erth) and sister of Saint Uny, Virgin;' adding that she lay in the parish church of the town of 'Seynt Hy,' and that her day was kept on the third of February.

Finally, in 1538, John Leland, when visiting St Ives, found a Latin life of the saint in the parish church, which has since been lost, and from it noted that St Ia, a disciple of St Barricus, and 'Elwine, with many other, cam into Cornewaul, and landid at Pendinas. This Pendinas is the peninsula and stony rok wher now the toun of St Ie's standith. One Dinan, a great Lord in Cornewaul, made a chirch at Pendinas, at the request of Ia, as it is writen yn St Ie's legende.'

When Gwinear set out on his journey, his objective was not Cornwall, but Brittany, where he is actually commemorated at Pluvigner, near Auray. Contrary winds, however, drove his party to the port called Huel (Hayle) where they found Ia already established. Gwinear and his companions marched across the river to Connerton, or Conner Downs, where they were all killed by Tewdrig, the local prince. St Ia appears not to have been involved in this massacre. According to a somewhat unreliable Breton source, however, she was born about 430 AD, converted to Christianity by 'Saint Patrice l'Ancient,' and martyred with 'Fingars' and 777 pious companions by 'Theodoric'.

At the place where St Hya landed she built for herself a rough cabin or oratory. The people among whom she settled were fishermen, and the little community, after accepting her Christian teaching, adopted also her name, the place then being known as Porthya or Porthia—Ia's cove. This was eventually anglicised to St Ie's; but in the 1571 Subsidy Roll the name is first found in its modern and corrupt form of St Ives. One can but speculate how the intrusive 'v' came to be inserted. There is certainly no connection between the Cornish St Ives and the one in Huntingdonshire, which is derived from an entirely different saint, a Persian Bishop Ivo, whose body, with those of two companions, was unearthed there about the year 1001. It should be noted, however, that the cult of St Ia is by no means confined to St Ives. There was formerly (in 1429) a chapel and holy well dedicated to her at 'Fenton Ear' in Troon, in the parish of Camborne. A cross which formerly stood there is now preserved in Camborne churchyard. St Hya may also be the eponym of the parish of Plouyé, near Carhaix, in Brittany.

After St Ia, complete silence descends on the history of Porthia for half a thousand years, until the Norman Conquest and the record of feudal land ownership made for William in the Domesday Survey. The parishes of St Ives, Towednack and Lelant then formed part of the royal manor of Connerton and the manor of Luduham (Ludgvan Leaze.)

Connerton was the paramount manor of the Hundred of Penwith, and with Ludgvan Leaze had probably been created long before the Conquest. Indeed, Charles Henderson was of opinion that Connerton, as a royal manor, may have represented the principality of Tewdrig, who slew Gwinear and the other martyrs. As late as 1659 Connerton claimed Are or Arthia (Ayr), Hendra, Hellisvean, Treloyan, Lidgiow (which cannot be identified) and Tregennowe as free tenements, its conventionary lands being Fower as Foyer, Treloyan and a grist mill near Porth Ia. The remainder of the parish seems to have been in Ludgvan

14

Leaze, and from it were created the later reputed manors of Porth Ia Prior, St Ives or Dinas Ia, St Ives and Treloyhan. The more ancient Corva Manor included Carnstabba in Polmanter. In Domesday, Connerton is credited with the possession of 7 hides of land and 40 ploughs, whilst the king had 30 villeins, 30 serfs and 20 bordars. Luduham had 3 hides and 15 ploughs, with 14 villeins and 40 bordars.

A curious relic of those distant manorial times survives at Bussow, Towednack, in a primitive-looking little 13th century columbarium or culver house, which stands remote from human habitation in the valley below Rosewall Hill. It is built of granite, the walls being extremely thick, and has a domed beehive roof of the same material. There is a low doorway; and small holes in the wall about 5 feet from the ground admitted the pigeons, which belonged to the lord of the manor—probably Ludgvan Leaze. These birds fed on grain grown by the tenants, but were destined for the lord's table!

During the 12th and 13th centuries the little settlement at the head of the Bay where St Uny, brother of St Ia, had established himself, and which was known as St Euny Lelant, grew into a place of some significance, both as a port with a custom house, and as a market, the latter granted by a royal charter of 1296. But this prosperity did not last. Its busy little harbour became choked with sand and alluvium, and its trade passed to St Ives, which began to develop during the 14th century from an insignificant village into a thriving little town, with separate parochial limits for fiscal and civic purposes. However, ecclesiastically, St Ives remained a part of the large parish of Lelant, and its inhabitants were obliged to journey to Lelant for baptisms and funerals, as they had always done.

This the townspeople considered a great hardship; and on September 27, 1409 Peter Pencors, William Stabba, James Tregethes, John Guvan and other parishioners of the chapels of St Tewennoc the Confessor (Towednack) and St Ya the Virgin, complained to the Bishop of Exeter that they lived, for the most part, four, three, or (at least) two miles from the mother church of Lananta (Lelant), the roads being mountainous and rocky, and liable, in winter, to sudden inundations, so that they could not safely attend Divine Service, or send their children to be baptised, their wives to be purified, or their dead to be buried. The children often went unbaptised, and the sick were deprived of the last Sacraments. They had built the chapels of Tewennoc and St Ya at their own expense, and enclosed suitable cemeteries, sufficiently endowed for two priests, and they prayed the Bishop to consecrate them.

The Bishop ordered an enquiry into these grievances. However, to reinforce their claim, the petitioners made a similar representation to the Pope, through Lord Champernowne, Lord of Ludgvan Leaze and High Lord of St Ives. Accordingly, on October 20, 1409 Pope Alexander V issued a Bull requesting the Bishop to make the chapels of St Tewynnocus and St Ya parochial, with fonts and cemeteries, but still subject to their mother church. Alexander died shortly afterwards, but John XIII, his successor, issued a similar Bull on November 28, 1410. However, John, the Vicar of Lelant and the vested interests which supported him successfully opposed this order, and all that the parishioners obtained by their costly efforts was a renewal by the Bishop of the licences previously granted to them for the celebration of mass and divine service (matins and evensong) in their respective chapels.

Undeterred by this failure, the people of St Ives applied successfully to the Archbishop of Canterbury and Bishop of Exeter for licences to build the magnificent 'chapel' with tower, which forms the present parish church of the town. It was begun in 1410, in the reign of King Henry V, and completed in 1426, taking 16½ years in building.

This splendid edifice thus symbolised the new-found civic pride of the people of St Ives and their determination to assert their independence. A subsequent Vicar of Lelant, Sir Richard Tresaghar, realising he would have to come to terms with this new situation, made a statesmanlike agreement with them, giving consent to the consecration of the Chapel of St Ya and its cemetery.

The text of the resulting *Composicio*, dated at Crediton 1 June 1429, was published by Canon Doble in his *St Ives, Its Patron Saint and its Church*. It contains several interesting pieces of information. Thus, the inhabitants of Porthia are described as 'for the most part sailors and unlearned, and the town of Porthia and the surrounding hamlets are near the sea, and in time of war the people are too far from Lanant to attend divine offices [to pray for] the King and the Realm.' In return for the consecration of their chapel, they acknowledged that the Church of St Ewinus should remain the mother church, and promised to contribute to its upkeep. They also agreed to observe the Feast of St Ewinus, together with the day (unfortunately not specified) of the dedication of the mother church and to attend divine service there on those occasions as hitherto. The Feast Day of St Ia would be celebrated as a principal feast on February 3. Also, in token of their now nominal subjection to the mother church, they were to bring to its high altar at the solemn mass on Easter Day 'a candle weighing 2 lbs of Wax, which shall always burn on divers feasts and holy days before the Gospel, and shall be called *The Candle of St Ya*.' Hicks, in his now lost *History of St Ives*, gave the date of the consecration of the new parish church as February 3, 1434, though this cannot be confirmed from any surviving document.

St Ives did not obtain the right to a cemetery of its own until 1542. Remaining differences between the two parishes were finally brought to an amicable conclusion in 1576 when a treaty was signed between the townsmen and the Vicar of Lelant by which the vicar agreed to keep a curate to serve the chapel of St Ives, and the townsmen promised to maintain the fabric of the chapel in repair, and to continue paying an annual tribute of £1 3s 8d to the mother church.

Although, with the dedication of its new church in 1434, St Ives had effectively broken the ecclesiastical fetters which bound it to Lelant, the townspeople were still obliged to resort to that place for their marketing. This was an obvious inconvenience; and so, in the third year of Henry VII (1488) Sir Robert Willoughby, afterwards Lord Broke, who had gained possession of the manor of St Ives by marrying the heiress of Lord Champernowne, acting on their behalf, obtained a charter for a weekly Saturday market with two annual fairs. A market house was erected two years later near the church and survived until 1832, when being decrepit it was taken down and replaced by the present structure. Lord Broke also erected and armed a fort to protect the town. This was built on a rock at the base of the present Smeaton's Pier, which thereafter became known as Castle Rock. This structure was still standing in 1745.

That such protection was badly needed in those troubled times had been well illustrated previously (in the reign of Henry VI, 1422-61) when four French ships which had previously sacked Marazion, landed at Porthminster, burned it to the ground and killed twenty men, afterwards sailing away with their booty. Porthminster thereafter remained uninhabited until the early 19th century, when a few cottages were built in the valley by the side of the stream.

In August 1497 Perkin Warbeck, the Pretender, and his wife, Lady Catherine Gordon, arrived at St Ives from Ireland with four ships of war and about 150 men, and was proclaimed as King Richard IV. He subsequently proceeded to St Michael's Mount where his wife was installed in the castle, whilst Perkin and his adherents marched towards Bodmin.

After the failure of his ill-starred enterprise he was taken and executed at Tyburn on November 23, 1499.

During the early 16th century St Ives was threatened by the fate which had previously brought disaster to Lelant—burial by sand. Leland, writing in 1538, stated: 'most part of the houses in the peninsula be sore oppressid or over covered with sandes that the stormy windes and rages castith up there. This calamitie hath continuid ther litle aboue 20 yeares. . . . The best part of the town now standith in the south part of the peninsula, toward another hille for defence from the sandes.'

In 1549, during the reign of the boy king Edward VI, St Ives and the whole of Cornwall was convulsed by the Prayer Book Rebellion. To further the objects of the Reformation, the government had ordered the old Latin service books to be abolished and replaced by the new English Prayer Book, and all images removed from the churches. Cornish was then the principal language spoken in the county, English being but little understood, and these changes were strongly resented. The Cornish people rose in revolt in defence of their old religion and form of service; and John Payne, the Portrieve or Mayor, became a captain in the rebel army.

This force marched into Devonshire under the leadership of Sir Humphrey Arundell, Governor of St Michael's Mount, and laid seige to Exeter. They spent six weeks before the city; and this delay gave Lord Protector Somerset time to gather the king's forces together; after a series of desperate encounters the Cornishmen were defeated by superior numbers and retreated across the Tamar. Had Arundell bypassed Exeter and marched straight on London there can be little doubt that he would have been victorious and restored England to the Catholic faith.

To ensure there was no further trouble in the far West, Somerset sent Sir Anthony Kingston, the Provost Marshal, to search out and punish such leaders of the rebellion as had not already been taken and executed. At Bodmin he hanged Boyer, the Mayor; and on arriving at St Ives was entertained with much ceremony at the old George and Dragon inn in the Market Place by John Payne, the Portrieve, who hoped his part in the affair had now been forgotten.

A little before dinner, Sir Anthony took the Mayor aside and whispered to him that an execution must be carried out that day in the town, and requested that a pair of gallows be erected by the time dinner should end. The Mayor was diligent in fulfilling this command, and no sooner was the meal over than the Provost demanded to know whether the work had been completed. The Mayor answered that all was ready. 'I pray you,' said the Provost, 'bring me to the place.'

'The Mayor,' runs the old tradition, 'therewith took him friendly, and beholding the gallows he asked the Mayor whether he thought them to be strong enough. 'Yes,' said the Mayor, 'doubtless they are.' 'Well,' said the Provost, 'get up speedily, for they are prepared for you.' 'I hope,' answered the Mayor, 'you mean not as you speak.' 'In faith,' said the Provost, 'there is no remedy, for you have been a busy rebel.' So presently the Mayor was hung up.' John Payne's arms, cut in one of the seats of the Parish Church, show two kneeling figures supporting a shield on which are the words 'John Peyn.'

Such commotions as this could not halt the steady progress of the town, and in 1558 Queen Mary recognised its growing importance by creating St Ives a Parliamentary Borough, with the right to send two members to Westminster. This proved to be a somewhat mixed blessing, for whilst it conferred on the place a status much envied by its less favoured neighbours, there came in its train those inevitable concomitants of a Cornish rotten borough—bribery, corruption and other malpractices. The first two members were Thomas Randolph (a Commissioner of the Exchequer) and William Chambre. Among their more distinguished successors were William Noye (1625), the Attorney General who originated the idea of levying ship-money; Edmund Waller (in the Long Parliament) the poet, nephew of Hampden and cousin of Cromwell; William Praed (1782), the banker, after whom Praed Street in London takes its name; and Edward Lytton Bulwer (1832), later Lord Lytton, the author. By the 1832 Reform Bill St Ives lost one of its two members; and the limits of the constituency have since been extended to take in all West Cornwall and the Scilly Isles, but its old name has not been changed.

St Ives was still subject to some feudal exactions and control well into the 16th century. This is well illustrated by the Penheleg manuscript of 1580, an 18th century transcript of which was discovered by P. A. S. Pool in 1955 and published in the *Journal* of the Royal Institution of Cornwall for 1959. This Ms comprises a statement of the royalties or franchises enjoyed by the Arundell family of Lanherne, as overlords of the Hundred of Penwith in right of their manor of Connerton between 1500-80. It is named after its author, John Penheleg, one of the officers employed by the Arundells to enforce their right of wreck in Penwith. Born *c*1514 at Illogan, he settled in 1568 at St Ives, of which place he became Town Warden in 1573-4.

Penheleg stated that in the 36th year of Henry VIII (1545) two Norman ships coming from Newfoundland with fish were obliged by stress of weather to anchor in St Ives Bay, where many of their men were drowned in attempting to reach the shore while the tempest still raged, eighteen being lost from one raft. England and France were then at war, but the survivors 'had pasport and went their ways.' When the weather moderated, the townsmen boarded the ships, which had ridden out the storm, and brought them within the quay. 'Then came the most part of the Gentlemen there about as Mr Godolphin Sentaben [St Aubyn] Reskymer Mylyton Nevyan [Vivian] Trewynard and many others more,' who took the fish from both ships, helped by the townsmen, and placed it in cellars.

However, before this work had been completed, Harry Bree, Sir John Arundell's bailiff, and John Penheleg went aboard the ships and arrested them with the remaining fish. They stayed on board for a week or more, but eventually were put out by the townsmen and others. The two agents went to Sir John, who was staying with a Mr Roskarrock, and complained of their treatment; he immediately sent his precept to St Ives to have the two town 'rulers' Thomas Jenkyn and John Stephen brought before him, and committed them to 'Launston Goal' for a month. Soon afterwards he sent three barks from Padstow under the command of Thomas Trevethan, gentleman, with one Jago and others, his servants and friends, reinforcing them by land with a hundred more, some having Henry VIII's commission to execute his warrant in the matter. The three barks and the hundred men met at St Ives, where Harry Bree demanded that the ships and fish be delivered up, but was refused by Thomas Godolphin, second son to Sir William Godolphin. Upon this, the doors of the cellars in which the fish had been stored were broken open, the fish loaded into the three barks and taken to Padstow for Sir John Arundell. The rest of the fish was given to his servants and friends, whilst the smaller ship (of 50 tons) was given to the townsmen, and the larger one (probably of 100 tons) sold to them. Sir John Arundell's right to the ships and their contents was subsequently confirmed at a Court of the Franchises held at Lelant Vicarage, 'and so he had the same quietly and so all other wracks sythence as Lord of the Franchise.' A curious verdict, seeing that the ships had not been wrecked at all, but merely abandoned by their crews!

18

The manor of Connerton exercised jurisdiction at St Ives in other ways. In 1568 James Cook (or Cock) then aged 90, giving sworn evidence touching the liberties of Connerton and the Hundred of Penwith appendant to it, declared that 'he did see a woman of Saint Ives which had committed murder upon Marin Bossenye and prisoned in Connerton Goal and at a Sessions kept there she was judged to be hanged: and because she committed the fact at Saint Ives by request of the towns men to the Justices she was carried to Saint Ives and there hanged for example upon the Island there at Saint Ives.' James Cook's testimony was confirmed by Richard Rosswall, aged 82, who added that the woman's name was 'Jowna.' He also saw when he was young a man brought from 'Conerton Goal' to St Ives and there hanged upon a gallows at 'Ardeca'—probably meant for 'Areeia,' or 'Arth Ya'—that is, Ayr. Both these executions must have taken place around the year 1500, perhaps earlier.

So far, we have been dependant on scattered records for our knowledge of the town's history; but in 1570 it is as if a window suddenly opens on the past, revealing in fascinating detail events and people of St Ives. The source of this information is the two volumes of the Borough Accounts, the first running from 1570 to 1638, and the second from 1638 to 1717, with scattered entries thereafter up to about 1832. The earlier of these documents, after being lost for many years, was discovered in 1890 by the late Sir Edward Hain amongst the sweepings of a solicitor's office; he arranged for the tattered and decayed manuscript to be carefully restored and rebound.

This book carries us back to the days of 'merry England,' before Puritan influences had made themselves felt, and there are some evocative allusions to those halcyon times when people joined easily and naturally in all kinds of innocent pleasures without a thought that they might thereby be doing wrong. Take, for example, the 'Summer Games' which were held annually at St Ives, doubtless on May Day and St John's Day, and in which the May-pole and other pleasant diversions figured prominently. These events were presided over by a King and Queen, chosen from among the handsomest lads and lasses of the town. They were the means of raising money, which the King and Queen handed over to the Mayor for the relief of the poor of the parish. Thus, in 1573 we read: 'Item rec: of the kinge and quene for the somer games. Ili 0s ivd.' The 'kinge and quene' that year were Henry Sterrie and Jane Walshe; the last known holders of these offices (in 1634) being John Stephens and Margery Hammande.

Another diversion much enjoyed by St Ives people in the 16th century was the Cornish Guary or Play. Richard Carew, in his *Survey of Cornwall* (1602) described the 'Guary Miracle' as an interlude compiled in Cornish out of some scripture history. 'For representing it, they raise an earthen Ampitheatre, in some open field, hauing the Diameter of his enclosed playne some 40. or 50. foot. The Country people flock from all sides, many miles off, to hear and see it: for they haue therein, deuils and deuices, to delight as well the eye as the eare: the players conne not their partes without booke, but are prompted by one called the Ordinary, who followeth at their back with the booke in his hand, and telleth them softly what they must pronounce aloud.' The dramas were acted, at one time, for several days together, and bore a close resemblance to the English mysteries of the same period.

The 'open field' where these guaries were performed at St Ives was at Little-in-Sight, about half-way up the Stennack valley. Though the valley has changed much since those far-off times, one can, without too much difficulty, visualise the setting of the amphitheatre here in a sunny meadow partly shaded by tall elms and with a distant view of the blue waters of the Bay and of the eastern shore.

Several entries in the Borough Accounts relate to the staging of guaries at St Ives, which clearly enjoyed the full backing and support of the town authorities. In 1573 there was 'receiued of John Clarke for ye enterlude, Ili xjd' with a further sixpence from 'Wm Trinwith for sixe score and thre foote of elme bordes in ye playing place.' From a series of entries in 1575 it would seem that performances of the play were given for six (presumably consecutive) days, the receipts varying from 12s on the first day to £4 10s 6d on the third, the total for the week being £14 15s 8d—a large sum of money in those days, and an indication of the plays' popularity. A further 2s 8d was received for 'drincke monye after the playe'! Perhaps the most curious of all the entries is the following, also from 1575: 'spent upon the carpenters yt made hevin iiijd.' Were 'elme bordes' ever put to a better purpose?

During the period covered by these accounts St Ives was governed by a body consisting of 12 capital and 24 common burgesses presided over by the Portrieve or Head Warden. A great deal of power and authority resided with them, for St Ives was then a remote and isolated community; though expected to pay its full quota of national taxes it was largely autonomous in the management of its own affairs. So the '12 and 24 men' as they were styled had to deal with all manner of business—repairing the church, controlling the fisheries, looking after the parish paupers, upholding the law and punishing offenders, enforcing public health regulations, collecting harbour dues, running the market, and also, most importantly in those warlike times, when the coast was always liable to attack by French, Spanish and Turkish vessels, taking active measures for the defence of the town.

Take first the case of poor relief. The authority maintained several 'Lazarus houses' where paupers were kept at public expense. In 1592 4s 6d was 'paide for a hundred and halfe of reede to thacke [thatch] the lazares houses and for ropes;' whilst in 1596 6s was given 'to a couple of women that shrowded ye lazar John Nyclis: and ther breake faste that tyme.' A good deal of out-relief was also provided. In 1575 various items of clothing were bought for the parish paupers. There is mention of 4s paid for 'iiij yeards & a quarter of Canves for harryes sherte & elizabethe argosyas smocke,' with smaller amounts (1s 6d each) for material and labour for smocks for 'dyos doghter' and 'alye derys,' these last being obviously children.

Such acts of charity were not confined to local people. St Ives at that period was the principal port of embarkation in the west for passage to Ireland, and many travellers, including soldiers, were given assistance when passing through the town. In 1586 there was 'paid John polkenhorne by the condessente of the Constables for certayne Iryshemen hosted at his house, iijs viijd,' and in 1592 a shilling was given 'to a man of Irelande that had his barke stollen by pirats.'

Misdemeanours were punished in a salutary and effective fashion. For scolds, there was the ducking stool. In 1603, Danyell Sprigge received 5s 5d 'for makinge the cuckinge stoole & all things therto belonginge.' Drunkards and thieves were usually dealt with by being incarcerated in the stocks; but one can only guess what lay behind this entry made in 1594: 'paide to Jenkine treuingy and philipe for waching [watching] of Henry Poter and his sonn in the stokes 2s and for makeinge of the metimas [mettimus] 6d.' The pillory served much the same purpose as the stocks, but was, if anything, even more uncomfortable, as one had to stand in an awkward position whilst undergoing punishment instead of sitting down. In 1617 3s 4d was given 'for a beame for the pillorye.' Another instrument of correction was the 'kaidge' or cage, which, with the stocks, pillory and whipping post, stood in the market place, probably between the market house and church tower. This was made in 1638, its cost including 4s for a beam, 1s 10d for a lock and key, 1s 6d for 'culleringe' (painting), and 12s to 'ye Carpenters.'

The townsmen's involvement with the church is well illustrated by a number of entries made in 1573. 'Paid to the parishe of Ste Unye for one year's rent, ili iiis viijd.' (This was the annuity paid to the mother church at Lelant). 'Payd for a barrell of lyme and vj bundells of lathes for to drese the Church vs vjd.' 'Payd to John Williams for helling stones [healing stones, slates] and lathe nayles for the church vs.' 'Paid for thre heliars' [slaters'] wages nine daies xjs iijd.' 'Paid to the glasiar for mendinge ye windowes vijs.' 'Paid for iij heliers' meate & drinke ix daies xs.' 'Paid for halfe a barrell of lyme for ye churche js.' Doubtless these repairs were necessitated by storm damage.

In matters of public health one of the greatest problems of those times was combating the plague, then endemic in Britain. Seaports such as St Ives were particularly susceptible to outbreaks of the disease owing to the constant arrival of rat-infested ships; and in September 1603 the town introduced a series of measures designed to obviate the danger. It was ordered that 'for the better provencion of the plague which by the visitacion of almightye god extreamelye raigneth in divers citties, townes, places and parishes (the lord in his greate mercye spedilye remove and staye it) and in Regard [that] diuerse persons aswell by sea as by land, may hereafter commynge from these places where the Sicknes and plague nowe is maye by ther accesse comyng nye to our towne or parishe of St Ies, endaunger our estats, and enthrall us in this mortalitye and sicknes,' any inhabitant providing accommodation for strangers from infected towns should be fined 8s 4d; and if any house became infected 'ther doares ar to be nayled up, and [the occupants] to be barred from common societye.' Persons arriving by sea from infected ports were to remain on board their ships, the fine for breach of this regulation being 13s 4d; they were, however, to 'have broughte them what they shall need or wante, that our towne or parishe shall yeld for the supplyinge ther necessities.' This order did not, however, succeed in keeping out the dread disease.

During the late 16th century the Cornish coast was subject to attack by Spanish ships, Mount's Bay suffering a severe raid of this kind in 1595. Following that incident, the St Ives authorities, fearful for their own safety, levied a rate to improve the local defences, but found some difficulty in collecting it. So, in the following year (1596) they ordered that those who had not paid 'the rate made through the hole towne and pry'she of St Yees in ano: 1595: . . . after attempt made by the Spanyards upon mowsholle, newlyn and penzans . . . for provision of ordenance, shott and powder and other muniments to resyst that Enimy; wh'che at that tyme . . . thretned the Rewyne of our towne' must pay their arrears towards the repair of the church windows and churchyard.

The defence arrangements which had been made involved dividing the town into eight parts, each placed under the command of a capital burgess, in order that 'bollworckes'' might be erected at 'pormeare' and other places, as required by Sir Francis Godolphin, the work to be carried out on Saturdays and at other times as directed by the head warden.

The Barbary Rovers (Turks) were also much feared by coast dwellers, and with reason. In 1635 a Turkish pirate of 12 guns and about 90 men was brought into St Ives harbour. This ship had previously taken three small vessels belonging to Looe and Fowey which were turned adrift and twelve men and two boys made prisoners. The Cornishmen managed to seize the ship whilst it was cruising in the Channel, the captain being knocked down with a capstan bar and thrown overboard. The other pirates were driven below, where they continued to fire shot through the deck whilst the escaped captives sailed their prize to St Ives. Here the ship was seized by the vice-admiral who maintained the Turks in the town for some months, and is supposed to have afterwards returned them to their own country.

ABOVE: The Bussow Columbarium; Halsetown in the distance. (WT);
BELOW: The 1296 Lelant charter. (Reproduced by permission of HM
Controller of the Stationery Office)
INSET: Zennor cromlech. (ETB)

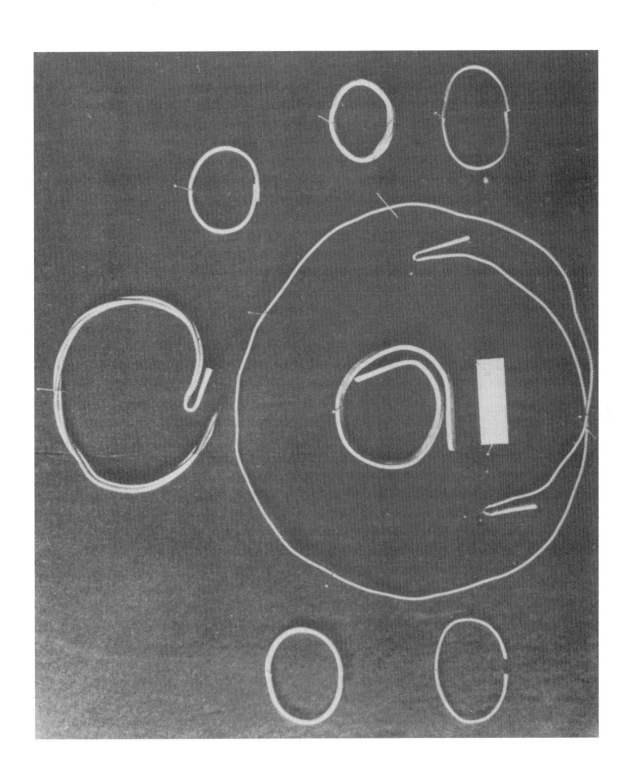

The Towednack gold hoard—the originals are in the British Museum. (M)

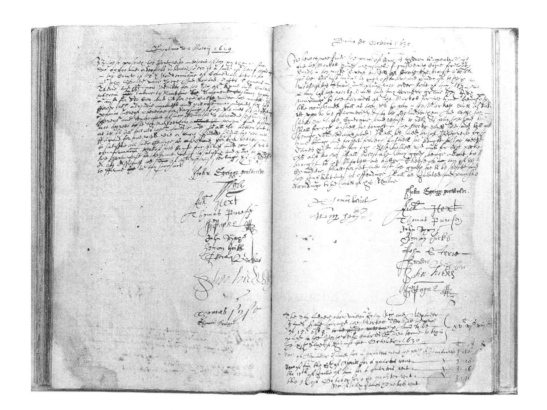

ABOVE: May 7, 1629 market lease rules, and October 10, 1630, corn tolls—
from the Borough Accounts (TC, WT); BELOW: The John Payne Memorial
outside the Catholic Church. (WT)

The Cure of Souls

The early 15th century parish church of St Ives is a handsome edifice whose 115 ft high tower dominates the central part of the town. Its principal features include the sandstone piers with richly carved capitals; magnificently carved and moulded wagon roof; granite font with representations of the demons cast out by baptism; and a series of bench ends carved by Ralph Clies, master smith, on which he portrayed himself and his wife, together with the tools of his trade. Granite for building the tower and church was brought by sea from Zennor, the boats often having to wait for weeks for sufficiently calm water. The Lady Chapel, or Trenwith Aisle, was added between 1450-1500; it contains a brass to Otho de Trenwith and his wife Agnes, the latter shown kneeling in effigy before St Michael. An inscription in Latin records that Otho died in the second year of Edward IV. The fine churchyard cross dates from the late 15th century.

During medieaval times St Ives possessed several little chapels in which Mass was said by the large staff of clergy then resident here. Tregenna, Porthminster and St Luke's chapels have now disappeared, but St Nicholas', on the Island, and St Leonard's, on the quay, still remain. St Nicholas' chapel, dedicated to the patron saint of sailors and of children, was demolished in 1904 by the War Office, who had been using it as a store and were ignorant of its ancient significance. Rebuilt by Sir E. Hain in 1911, the building was further restored by the late J. F. Holman and reopened with a service on December 6, 1971—St Nicholas' day—and has since been visited by thousands of people.

St Leonard's, on the quay, was the fishermen's chapel. After a chequered career, it was also restored by Mr Holman and reopened on June 13, 1974. The blocked east window and stone altar supports of the original structure are still to be seen. It contains a bronze memorial to St Ives fishermen who lost their lives at sea.

A Mariners' Chapel, for the use of fishermen and their families, was opened in the lower part of St Ives in August 1867, and was replaced in 1905 by a much larger church intended as a memorial to Canon J. B. Jones, a former Vicar of St Ives. This is now an art gallery.

Around 1830 James Halse laid out the mining village of Halsetown near St Ives on a 'garden city' plan to house his numerous workpeople, one of its early residents being young Johnny Broadribb, better remembered as Sir Henry Irving, the great Victorian actor-manager. In 1846 Halsetown was constituted a separate parish, and a temporary chapel was opened in the upper part of the village in 1847. A new parish church, designed by J. P. St Aubyn, known as St John's in the Fields, was built on a site near Hellesvean about a mile distant from the village it was intended to serve, all the land near Halsetown being owned by Nonconformists. They refused, for sectarian reasons, to sell any ground for the purpose! St John's was consecrated on May 26, 1860. Robert Hichens, James Halse's brother-in-law, provided the endowment, and the Rev W. H. Drake was appointed the first incumbent. Access was gained to the village in 1878 with the opening of St Mary's Mission

Church in what had formerly been a Teetotal Methodist Chapel; this has since been closed. The Rev T. C. F. Barfett, instituted as Vicar in 1915, was a remarkable personality who will be long remembered by his parishioners. A keen gardener, he rode a motorcycle about the district when well into his 80's. At the time of his death in 1968 he had held the living for over half-a-century. His successor, the Rev J. H. Harper, has effected many innovations, including the resiting of the altar in the centre of the church.

Lelant Parish Church, standing at the edge of the sand dunes beneath which lie buried the houses of old Lelant Town, is essentially at 15th century building, but incorporates remains of earlier work—in particular, the Norman arch and font. The beautiful windows in the south aisle are particularly worthy of note. The name 'Lelant' is derived from 'Lan-Anta,' *lan* meaning monastery and *Anta* a saint's name. The church itself was dedicated to St Uny, brother of St Ia and St Erth. In 1495 a Chapel of St Anta 'on the sea shore' in this parish was maintained by a Gild. This chapel apparently stood on or near the rock called Chapel Anjer at the mouth of Hayle River, and a harbour light may have been kept there to guide shipping through the dangerous channel to the busy port within.

Around 1170 Thomas Beket, Archbishop of Canterbury, confirmed the Church of St Euni to the Priory of Tywardreath. This confirmed two previous charters, the first by Robert fitz William, lord of the manor of Ludgvan Leaze, to which the advowson had apparently been attached, and the second, *c*1150, by Robert de Cardinham. The church was subsequently acquired by Bishop Bronescombe, who in October 1272 appropriated it to the collegiate church of Crediton in exchange for the church of Egloshayle, and the cure of souls became a vicarage.

After the long struggle between Lelant and the parishes of St Ives and Towednack had resulted in the inhabitants of those places gaining the right to sepulture in 1429 and 1542 respectively, the Vicars of Lelant removed to St Ives, where they remained for the next three centuries, whilst the old vicarage fell into ruins and the church to decay. A thorough restoration of the latter was carried out in 1873.

In addition to Chapel Aanjer, there were several ancient chapels in the parish, at Trembethow, Brunnion and Trevarrack. Lelant is particularly rich in ancient crosses, not less than ten still surviving, and the sites of others can be inferred from a study of old place names. The interesting building at Lower Lelant known as the Abbey, originally forming three sides of a square, one of which was demolished during the last century, is said to have been the residence of the pre-Reformation clergy at Lelant.

Towednack Parish Church, in its remote moorland setting, is remarkable for having a short, squat tower. The local explanation for this curious feature is that when the masons were building it the devil came every night and carried off the pinnacles and battlements until at length they gave up the work in despair. Alone among the churches of West Cornwall Towednack possesses a 13th century chancel arch acutely pointed. The building contains several interesting early features, including a granite altar slab, and a stone with an incised cross of the Celtic period, possibly indicating that Towednack only became subject to Lelant after the Conquest. Towednack Church was made parochial at the same time as St Ives, but was not finally separated from Lelant until 1902. Since 1947 the church has been run in plurality with Zennor. The dedication is to St Winwaloe, a Breton saint.

In 1907 the Rev W. R. Erskine, Vicar of Lelant, realised that the growing population of Carbis Bay would eventually necessitate the building of a parish church there, and made plans to that end. Services began in Mr Payne's large tea room on Sunday afternoons in 1910, and in the following year a small wooden mission church was built—this is now

Trevorrow's shop, opposite Carbis Bay church. An anonymous gift of £7,000 enabled the foundation stone of the church to be laid on September 15, 1927, and the building was dedicated on May 9, 1929. The Rev (now Canon) A. S. Roberts was inducted as first Vicar of the Church of St Anta and All Saints, Carbis Bay, on December 18, 1948 by the Lord Bishop of Truro (Dr J. W. Hunkin), the consecration also taking place at this time. The tower and nave were completed in 1959 and 1968, the final consecration being performed on June 16 of the latter year. For the final stages stone was obtained from an old building of Wheal Sisters mine at Trencrom. The church, in the English Gothic style, was designed by Mr Wheatley.

The church of the primitive, unspoiled moorland parish of Zennor was built about 1450, but parts of the south wall near the doorway are older, possibly of Norman date. The earliest reference to it was in 1150, when Ralph de Sicca Villa granted the sanctuary to Tywardreath Priory; but in 1270 Zennor was appropriated by Bishop Bronescombe to his newly founded Glasney College, near Penryn. The font, of Caen stone, may have been a gift from Glasney, where this material was largely employed in the buildings. There is a memorial outside the church to John Davey (d 1891), said to have been the last person who had any traditional knowledge of the Cornish language. Zennor church is dedicated to the female St Senara. Its most celebrated feature is the bench end (now a seat) carved with the figure of a mermaid holding a looking glass and a comb. Legend tells how she came up from the cove below the village to listen to the beautiful singing of Matthew Trewhella, the squire's son, in the choir, and enticed him away to live with her beneath the waves in Pendour Cove. There were two ancient chapels at Zennor; one, near Gurnard's Head (Chapel Jane) also had a holy well, which has been lost through cliff erosion.

The great evangelist John Wesley first visited St Ives on August 30, 1743, where a Methodist Society had already been established. He was well received at first; but on later visits encountered bitter hostility from the townspeople, incited by the preaching of Mr Hoblin, the Vicar, and Mr Symonds, the curate; but within two years he had so won them over that he called St Ives 'the most still and honourable post (so are the times changed) which we have in Cornwall.'

One of Wesley's strongest supporters was John Nance, who lived in Street-an-Garrow. His house was attacked by the mob when Wesley was preaching there to the infant Society. The site of the present Wesley Church was then John Nance's garden, and a meeting house was erected in its north-east corner. Mr Nance leased the ground to the Society, but they later obtained full possession, and in 1785 built their first chapel there, extending towards Chapel Street. This subsequently underwent several enlargements. On October 16, 1825 it was reopened after such an extension. The roof was supported by massive pillars erected through the generosity of Mr Roger Wearne, who asked all his seiners to come up to place them in position and fix a heavy girder above, free of cost. In the 1890's these rather unsightly pillars were removed and the roof rebuilt with steel girders, on the same principle as that used in the roofs of large railway stations.

In 1824 the St Ives Society opened a meeting house known as Mount Zion Chapel in the lower part of the town; this later became J. R. Cothey's boatbuilding workshop.

Halsetown Chapel was opened in 1833 and has only quite recently (in 1976) been closed. The chapel at Lower Lelant dates from 1834, a new bell turret being added in 1869. A small Wesleyan chapel was built at Carbis Water around 1835, replaced by a larger building on nearly the same site in 1885—this is now a nursing home. Carbis Bay Wesleyan Chapel, built to a somewhat unusual Gothic design, with a tower, by Oliver Caldwell, was opened by Miss Kitty Hain in July 1903. The stained glass windows in the main front were given by Dolcoath miners in memory of their late manager, Capt Josiah Thomas.

Polpeor Chapel, in the valley to the west of Trencrom, now a dwelling house, dates from 1872. A quaint old Weslyan chapel at Lelant Downs was completely remodelled in 1873; it is now closed. In 1844 a small chapel was built at Hellesveor, by the side of Consols pool. The closed chapel at Trezelah, near Badger's Cross, was removed piecemeal and re-erected at Hellesveor in 1937, the old chapel then becoming the Sunday school. The aptly-named Coldharbour Chapel in Towednack dates from 1844; it was once numerously attended, but the declining population led to its recent closing, and it is now a forlorn and desolate object. At Nancledra, a Wesleyan Sunday school was established in 1836 in the miller's barn, but the chapel was not built until 1844. A school was added later, being rebuilt in 1910.

John Wesley visited the parish of Zennor, staying in a cottage at 'Rosemargay,' where he had the use of 'a little chamber, and set for him there a bed, and a table, and a stool, and a candlestick.' An old Zennor prayer leaders' plan, dated 1840, lists meeting places at 'Chapel [ie, Churchtown], Trendrine, Porthmear, Bosprenis, Boswednack, Treen, Tremeader and Foge'. Sadly, all are now extinct.

During the first half of the 19th century various groups seceded from the Wesleyan Methodists. One of these, the Bryanites (so named after their leader, William O'Bryan) or Bible Christians, built a chapel in St Peter's Street in 1824, which was greatly enlarged in 1858. There were other Bible Christian chapels at Halsetown, Lady Downs and Tregerthen, the last now a picturesque ruin beside the St Ives-Zennor footpath.

Another group, the Primitive Methodists, made their appearance at St Ives in 1829. They first met in the open air, on the quay, then in Quick's sail loft; finally, a large chapel, the present Fore Street Methodist Church, was erected on the harbour in 1831. Blue elvan 'bowlies' (sea-rounded rocks) for building it were brought by fishing boat from Porthmeor Cove, near Gurnard's Head, and carried by women in their aprons to the site. However, most of the stonework is granite.

The Primitive Methodists subsequently built other chapels in the district. The earliest, opened 1835, closed 1896, was Trevalgan. Next came Lelant (1859-1909—it is now the village hall); Balnoon (1862-1888); Lady Downs; Nancledra (opened 1855); Trenwith (closed 1873); Longstone (1873-6); Chyangweal (c1856); Lelant Downs (c1865); Wheal Reeth (closed 1874); and Castle Gate (1873-1882). Ninnis Bridge (opened 1873) still survives. Georgia, or Towednack South, in the Penzance Primitive circuit, opened 1855, was known as Billy Bray's chapel, this well-known miner-evangelist having sometimes preached there; rebuilt 1888, it was finally closed in 1914, as a result of rural depopulation.

Another group of Methodists broke away from the parent Society at St Ives in 1838 on the total abstinence question, and formed a Teetotal Society. The Teetotal Chapel in Chapel Street was opened in 1842. They later built chapels at Sheffield, near Paul, in 1856, and at Polmanter Water, Halsetown, in 1844, the latter reopened in 1878 as St Mary's Mission Church. The circuit joined the New Connexion in 1860. In 1861-2 the Rev William Booth (later General Booth of the Salvation Army) conducted a successful 'revival' at the St Ives chapel. This building was closed in 1899 and became a Drill Hall, its members moving to an imposing new building at the bottom of Bedford Road. There was also an old New Connexion chapel at Carbis Bay, the present building at Chyangweal dating from 1901.

In the autumn of 1775 Selina, Countess of Huntingdon, visited St Ives and established a preaching room which, according to tradition, was situated at the foot of Barnoon Hill.

We learn from Wesley's *Journal* that the movement initiated by her young preachers did not last; but in 1786 she sent the Rev Robert McAll, who was more successful. In 1804 he converted an old fish cellar on the western side of Fore Street into a chapel; and whilst it was being built he conducted open-air meetings, preaching by the light of a candle held by young Andrew Noall in the streets and in the old Market House. The chapel he built is still in use.

The Salvation Army was established at St Ives in July 1879 by Capt Hanson. Their headquarters were in Jennings's sail loft at Market Strand; destroyed by fire in 1915, the present barracks were erected soon after on its site.

Following the establishment of a Roman Catholic mission at St Ives, mass was first publicly celebrated here in February 1902, after a lapse of centuries, in a room at Street-an-Pol. The property acquired by the mission extended down Street-an-Pol from Tregenna Place to a warehouse which has since become the Christian Science meeting room and offices, the Catholic chapel being situated in an upper room of this warehouse. When, after a few years, the present Catholic church was built at the top of Tregenna Hill, the Street-an-Pol property was sold, and Mr Cogan, who then ran a boot and shoe shop in what had formerly been Permewan's, at the Tregenna Place corner, reluctantly vacated these premises, which then became a chemist's. The Roman Catholic Church of the Sacred Heart and St Ia was opened in September 1908. Its walls are built of Trelyon Downs stone, with dressings of Cornish granite. The copper-covered turret spire and red tiled roof give the building a quite distinctive appearance. These red tiles and brickwork upset some of the artists and inhabitants, who asserted that they clashed with the traditional grey roofs and granite of the town. It is still the only red-roofed building in St Ives. The Rev A. J. Canon Scoles and B. G. Raymond were the architects, the builder being R. J. Sandrey. In the Catholic Hall may be seen what is probably the only gallery of pictures painted by Catholic artists (parishioners) owned by any parish in the country. Formed in 1941, it includes a terra-cotta head of Our Lady, modelled and given by Mrs Clare Sheridan, first cousin of Sir Winston Churchill. To mark the fourth centenary of the Cornish rising of 1549 a bronze and marble memorial tablet, designed by monks of Buckfast, was placed outside the church in 1949 to John Payne the mayor and others of St Ives who died with him. It was unveiled and blessed by the Bishop of Plymouth in the presence of the current Mayor, also named John Payne—a remarkable coincidence. The Rev Austin W. Delaney, OSB, who at the time of his retirement in 1973 had been the parish priest for 35½ years, was a much liked and respected personality, and the Freedom of the Borough was conferred on him that same year in recognition of his many services to the town and the high esteem in which he was held.

St Ives Parish Church and St Andrew's Street in the 19th century—the
white pole marks the boundary of a seine stem. (M)

ABOVE: The Trenwith brass, in the parish church; and
BELOW: the church inside, c1912.

ABOVE: St Nicholas Chapel, The Island, before restoration (M), and
LEFT: Building the churchyard wall, 1909. (HF; EA) RIGHT: 15th century angels, parish church.

ABOVE: Halsetown (WT)—Sir Henry Irving (INSET) (M) lived with his
aunt and uncle Penberthy in the corner house, and once rode through the
Inn passage on a donkey. BELOW: New Connexion (once Teetotal)
Chapel, Chapel Street—Harvest Festival, 1896. (TMB)

Back (left to right)—Delve, T. Grenfell, P. B. Stevens, R. Q. Stevens, J. Tanner, M. Couch, Martha White, M. White, L. Berriman, Harold Jenkin, Johns, F. E.
Jenkin, M. Phillips, E. Phillips, Berriman, Langford, unknown clarionettist, M. Jennings, M. Banfield, W. H. Jenkin. Front row—J. Daniel snr, A. Trewhella,
E. Ninnis, Mrs Wright, Rev Wright, Mrs E. P. Curnow, L. E. Comley, J. Daniel jnr, Mrs Chirgwin, Capt J. Stevens.

ABOVE: Lelant Church and INSET: Towednack Church; LEFT: the
headstone in Zennor church to John Quick who 'excel'd his equals'
and RIGHT: the Zennor mermaid. (All WT)

ABOVE: Cleaving Paal Maal beside Towednack road near Bussow reservoir, 1910; BELOW: Open air service nearby at Wesley's Rock, near Hellesveor Chapel, c1925. (RIC)

ABOVE: Two foundation stones were laid in 1885 at the new Zion Chapel
frontage by F. W. Willcocks of London and Dr Carne Ross of Penzance
(EA); BELOW: Lelant Methodist Chapel. (HF; EA)

ABOVE: Early Salvationists at Jennings' Sail Loft, Market Strand (destroyed by fire in 1915) (EA); LEFT: Bedford Road Church (M) and RIGHT: Brass banner pole insignia, found in Jennings' Sail Loft. (M; WT)

Title page of the second volume of the Borough Accounts, 1638. (TC; WT)

Within the Burrough

In 1639 Sir Francis Bassett, of Tehidy, who possessed considerable business interests at St Ives, and between whom and the local community had grown up strong feelings of mutual goodwill, exerted his influence upon Charles I, to procure a new Charter for the town. Sir Francis may also have had a secondary motive, for he cannot have failed to notice the rise of Puritan and Parliamentary sympathies among the principal inhabitants, and possibly hoped to check this and bind St Ives to the Royalist cause during the impending Civil War. If such were his object, he must have been bitterly disappointed for St Ives, almost alone among the intensely Royalist Cornish boroughs, opted for Parliament in that great struggle.

However, when the Charter was granted, the occasion was marked by every outward sign of harmony and satisfaction. Some of the entries in the second volume of the Borough Accounts, which commenced at about the same period, accurately reflect this feeling: 'Spent at Captaine Bassetts coming into our Towne from Sillye, 2s 0d.' 'Payd for sending of post Letters to Mr Bassett 1s 6d.' 'Payd for carrienge of Letters to Mr Bassett about Townes business 1s 6d.' 'Given at Mr Bassetts howse 14s 6d.' (That is, money disbursed to Mr Bassett's servants, at Tehidy, where the Corporation were regularly entertained at Christmas.) 'Spent att Mr Hammonds when ye charter was brought, 5s 6d.'

Sir Francis commemorated his success in procuring the Charter by presenting to the borough a beautiful silver loving cup—still one of the town's most prized possessions. The servant who took it to St Ives was handsomely rewarded for his trouble: 'Given to Mr Robert Arundle when he brought the cupp given by his Maister to our Towne, £2.' The cup is of solid silver, gilded within, elaborately chased and wrought. The hall marks are obliterated, with the exception of a lion passant; its date has been computed at about 1620. It measures $22\frac{3}{4}$ inches from base to top; the diameter of the cup itself is $7\frac{3}{4}$ inches, whilst from the base to the top of the head of the figure on the cover the height is 33 inches. This elegantly modelled dominating figure in armour has the left hand resting on a shield engraved with the crest of Bassett, whilst the right grasps a spear or bow. It stands on an oval ball and a three-sided pyramid, supported on three sea-horses. The cup's body, trumpet foot and cover are embossed with conventional foliage. A rim has been added to the top of the bowl at a later date to increase its capacity. Incised on the inside, and running around the base of the cup on the rim or splayed-out fringe on which it stands appears the charming and often-quoted inscription:

Iff any discord twixt my frends arise
Within the Burrough of Beloved St Ives
Itt is desyred that this my Cupp of Loue
To Everie one a Peace maker may Prove
Then am I Blest to haue giuen a Legacie
So like my hartt vnto Posteritie
Fcis Bassett Ano 1640.

It became the custom, on solemn occasions, for the cup to be handed round and the contents sipped by the Mayor and Aldermen, or a draught of mulled wine was presented in it to distinguished guests. Also, by an old custom, the children of St Ives were allowed a drink from the cup on Mayor's Day.

The Charter, the original of which has unfortunately been lost, made St Ives a municipality, with a mayor, recorder, town clerk, and a corporation consisting of twelve aldermen and twenty-four burgesses. It also confirmed all privileges granted to the town by previous sovereigns. The last person to hold office as Portrieve under the old dispensation was Mr Thomas Stevens, in 1638, the first Charter Mayor (1639) being Mr Richard Hext, 'gentleman.' Mr Hext commemorated the honour which had been conferred on him by presenting the new Corporation with a handsome and practical gift—a pair of heavy silver maces, the traditional symbols of civic authority. They bear the date 1641, with Richard Hext's name. Together, they weigh 5½ lbs; each is chased and engraved with the coat of arms of the Borough on top, and female figures in repousse pierced work round the head. The maces are badly dented, as though they had been vigorously used as weapons or to restore order!

The decision by St Ives to oppose the King during the Civil War may be partly attributed to the harsh treatment meted out by Royalist commander, Sir Richard Grenville, to all those he believed to be sympathetic towards Parliament; the main reason seems to have been that the principal leaders of opinion in the town were all staunch Puritans. Foremost among these was Major Peter Ceely, who had demonstrated his zeal for the cause by destroying the ancient chapel at Madron Well. The Stevens family of Tregerthen (later Stephens of Tregenna), who were Independents, and the wealthy Sises, merchants, also threw the full weight of their considerable influence against the King.

At the beginning of the war, however, St Ives was rated for the maintenance of the Royalist army in Cornwall, having to furnish a daily supply of 46 lb of bread, 40 lb of butter, 30 lb of cheese, 30 lb of beef and 50 lb of bacon. This was quite a heavy impost for such a small place, and must have been paid grudgingly by the local Roundheads. Even as late as 1645, the Corporation, still overawed by the military domination of the King's forces in Cornwall, were obliged to entertain visiting Royalist leaders at the town's expense: '[Spent] in meat and wyne upon Sir ffrancis Bassett, Sir ffrancis Molsworth and their followers with the brethren £2 2s 9d.' 'More wyne upon Sir Rich: Grenvill with the brethren 9s.' 'More Spent on my Lord Hopton and his followers with consent of the brethen £1 1s 3d.' Sir Ralph Hopton was a cavalry commander, and successfully held Cornwall for the King.

But the St Ives men bided their time; and that same year, seizing what they thought was a favourable opportunity to display their true sentiments, assembled on Longstone Downs with the men of Towednack and Zennor, about 200 in all, under the command of Capt Francis Arundell. Sir Richard Grenville marched against them with 600 horse and foot soldiers; and the St Ives Parliamentarians, finding themselves hopelessly outnumbered, scattered in different directions and through such bye-ways that no horse could overtake them; consequently only three or four on both sides were killed. The Royalists afterwards entered the town, and Sir Richard lodged at the house of the Mayor, Edward Hammond. For failing to keep his rebellious people in order, that dignitary was fined £500, and for refusing to pay it was sent to Launceston gaol, from where, after three months, he was released by order of Prince Charles. Before Sir Richard Grenville left the town, with characteristic harshness he ordered Phillips, a constable of Zennor, to be hanged, and the next day ordered a St Ives man to be hanged at Helston, whilst another suffered a similar fate at Truro. Capt Arundell was proclaimed a traitor and commanded to be hanged whenever taken, but, according to Hicks, he escaped from St Ives to Bridgwater and there joined Fairfax's army.

The St Ives men gave a better account of themselves later, when a Royalist army under Col Goring marched on the town. They stopped up the roads with pilchard hogsheads (casks) filled with sand, and maintained such a strong guard that the King's forces were obliged to retire to Penzance. One of these hastily contrived barricades is said to have been thrown across the Stennack.

The war ended with complete victory for Parliament; on January 30, 1648, the day when Charles I was beheaded in Whitehall, a ship riding in St Ives Bay with his wardrobe and other property aboard, though bound for France, was driven on the rocks of Godrevy Island in a great storm. She held about 60 persons, all of whom were drowned, except a man and a boy, who, with a wolf-dog, swam to the island and there subsisted for two days on rainwater and seaweed. When the storm abated they were rescued and brought to St Ives, where Mr Hicks, the historian, conversed with them.

Though St Ives suffered only minor casualties and apparently no damage in the war, it experienced in full measure a calamity of another kind which claimed the lives of no less than 535 of its inhabitants, or a third of the population of about 1,500 during the summer of 1647.

This was the plague, to escape which half the people fled from the town. The markets were closed, and the neighbouring farmers, afraid to come in with provisions, brought supplies to either side of the parish and left them beside the streams at Polmanter and Carbis Valley with their prices affixed. The inhabitants later took these supplies away, leaving their money in the streams to be purified by the water. In this way all risk of transmitting the disease was avoided. The Stephens family escaped the contagion by shutting themselves up in their farm at Ayr, so avoiding all communication with the town. It is probable that more would have died of hunger than the plague had not a vessel belonging to Mr Opye of Plymouth laden with wheat and butts of sack arrived unexpectedly in the harbour. The Mayor purchased the cargo for £196, the wheat was distributed gratis and the wine at 12s per quart.

Several entries in the Borough Accounts refer to this incident: 'Received att sevuerall tymes of Mr George Hicks for Corne monie £142 11s 4d.' 'More of Mr George Hicks upon Major Ceelye Tickatts for corne £4 11s 6d.' 'More of Mr Henrie Sterrie for a collection in St Iust parish, £1 17s 8d.' 'Received of Mr Hammond for a Butt of the Towne sacke £18.' 'Received of Mrs Newman for 3 butts of sacke and parte of a 4th that shee drew £80 7s 5d.'

Two traditions of the plague have not been recorded before. The late R. J. Noall asserted that the place used by Zennor people for leaving food and cattle was a field at Trevalgan called 'The Plague', situated near the St Ives parish boundary and which formerly comprised part of the lands leased by the Stevens family of Trevalgan. The St Ives people did not bring their money to this field, but placed it in a trough at Trevalgan farm. 'And there,' stated Mr Noall in 1906, 'is the very trough at Trevalgan today, now re-cut and used as a water trough at the village pump . . . It is strange that this should not have been mentioned in a (printed) history, although the tradition is well-known to the people of the place.' Again, some years ago, when excavations were being carried out under a building at the western end of High Street a quantity of human remains was discovered, but not reported to the authorities. As no record exists of a designated cemetery here, it seems a fair conclusion that this must have been the plague pit situated outside what were then the town limits, where infected corpses were buried to avoid the further spread of contagion. During this terrible plague year St Ives suffered another minor misfortune when a ship called the *James* fitted out by the merchants for the West Indies was captured by the Spaniards on her homeward voyage and sent to Spain.

During the Commonwealth the Puritan leaders of St Ives with Major Ceely at their head ruled the district with a rod of iron, in alliance with other Parliamentarians, such as the St Aubyn family, who had gained possession of St Michael's Mount from the Bassetts as a result of the war. In 1653, on the proclamation of Cromwell's protectorship, Hicks tells us that 'every soldier wore round his hat two yards of ribbon, one white, the other blue, and several hogsheads of beer were given to drink the old rebel's health.'

Major Ceely was appointed vice-admiral of the district by Cromwell, and also commanded a troop of horse—proving that the 'Horse Marines' may have been no mere fiction at that time! In 1654, Thomas Purefoy, who commanded a small privateer of four guns belonging to Ceely, captured and brought into St Ives two fine Breton barques laden with salt. Major Ceely may well have been responsible for removing the large organ in St Ives church. This was probably the first organ erected in Cornwall and is said to have cost £300. The entry, dated 1647, in the Borough Accounts relating to this reads: 'Payd the Joyners for takinge downe the Organs and Railings [rood screen] of the church £1 15s 7d.'

The Quakers were active during this period, but met with much persecution from the authorities. In 1656 George Fox, founder of the sect, and others of his persuasion were arrested for distributing tracts at St Ives and committed to Launceston gaol, their removal costing the town £1 2s. A year later William Ackland stabbed John Tackabird over a game of cards, and was hanged. His property was confiscated by the Corporation, as permitted by their Charter, realising a net sum at £4 5s 3d. His house was likewise forfeit, but his widow was permitted to continue living there, paying £2 annual rent. Ackland seems to have been a person of some standing, and at the time of his execution rented the market house tolls from the Council for a yearly sum of about £50. This is one of the few recorded murder cases at St Ives.

Oliver Cromwell died September 3, 1658, and on the 11th 3s was given 'to the gunners and drumer att the proclayminge the Lord Richard His highnesse [Cromwell's son] Lord Protector of the Common Wealth,' and 12s 'for beere for the Ringers and others that daye.'

Richard's Protectorship proved short lived. John St Aubyn and Peter Ceely were elected to represent St Ives in the last Commonwealth Parliament which met on January 29, 1659. On May 8, 1660 Charles II was proclaimed king; and the erstwhile St Ives Roundheads celebrated the event with apparently as much enthusiasm as they had recently marked the great events of the Commonwealth: 'Spent when the Newes came that the Kinge and Parliament was agreed By the Maior and brethren £1 10s 0d.' 'Spent then on the Ringers att John Hawkings house 15s 0d.' 'Spent when Mr Bassett was in Towne 5s 0d.' 'Payd Morrish Dyer ffor powder the same day 8s 0d.' 'Spent at Pollards house the day the Kinge was proclaymed 15s 0d.' 'Spent att John Hawkings the day aforesaid one barrell of beere at 15s 0d.' 'Spent the same on the Ringers 10s 0d.' At the coronation, 2s 6d was given to 'Cockin to beate the drume,' whilst further considerable sums were spent on beer. Also, 'paid for cutting the Kings Armes in the mace 4s 0d.' In such wise was the ghost of King Oliver laid at St Ives.

Quiet times then ensued for a number of years, though one frequently catches in the Borough Accounts echoes of great national events, such as the declaration of war by England and France against Holland in 1672 and the 'Popish Plots' in 1680, when two men were paid 5s 'to goe to Penzance & Penryn to discover a Jesuite.'

In 1682 a writ of Quo Warranto was issued by Charles against every Corporation in Great Britain, requiring the surrender of their charters, these being only restored on the payment of large sums of money. The Corporations were also required to choose the MP's prescribed for them. In this way St Ives was obliged to give up its 1639 Charter, which was duly returned, but a new one was granted by James II in 1685.

This constituted St Ives a Free Borough Incorporate, consisting of a Mayor, Recorder, Town Clerk, ten Aldermen and ten Common Councillors. They had power to hold a quarterly Sessions of the Peace, and to return two burgesses to Parliament; two markets were granted for Wednesday and Saturday, and four fairs on May 10, July 20, September 26 and December 3, each of two days. They also had power to hold a Court of Piepowder at the markets and fairs; to levy tolls, stallage and pickage at the markets and fairs; and to hold a Petty Sessions of the Peace every third Thursday. The Mayor was appointed Keeper of the Borough Gaol. Permission was given to levy quay dues, with tonnage, lestage, keelage and groundage, also tolls of fish.

The earliest surviving Borough Seal dates from the time of William and Mary, and was presented to the Corporation by Mr Praed of Trevetho. It is of silver, about $2\frac{1}{2}$ inches in diameter, with a handle of curiously blown glass. Circular in shape, it bears on a shield with scroll work at its sides and top the ivy branch arms of the town, together with the inscription: 'Sigillum Burgi St Ives in Com: Cornub: 1690.' After two centuries of use this seal began to show signs of wear; and so in 1890 the Mayor, Mr Edward Hain, presented a new lever-type embossing press as a replacement. The town arms on the 1690 seal do not represent the earliest surviving example of that device, those engraved on the maces being quite a few years older. There must also have been an older seal, or seals, with these arms, as is made quite clear by an entry dated 1650 in the Borough Accounts, where it was recorded that among the items handed over by the outgoing to the new Mayor were 'The Towne Seale and 2 stamps.' Heraldically, the town arms may be described as 'argent, an ivy-bush proper, overspreading the whole field.' The ivy was chosen as a supposed pun on 'Ives.' The Cornish historian Davies Gilbert stated in 1838 that these arms had 'afforded an obvious joke throughout the neighbouring parishes at the expense of the Mayor.' This joke, now long forgotten, was an allusion to that dignitary as 'the owl in the ivy bush.' It seems possible, however, that the ivy may have had a more serious significance than has been generally supposed; for it will be recalled that St Ia sailed over from Ireland on a leaf. At one period another device was used as a symbol for the town, about whose punning intent there could be no doubt whatever; this consisted of two bee-hives engraved on the sun-dial of the parish church tower.

The town was visited by a great storm in 1697, when a Dutch ship and the Expedition packet, from Lisbon, commanded by Capt Clies, were chased into St Ives Bay by a French privateer, which being fired on by the Castle guns, tacked about, and on her departure fired several shots into the town. One of these struck a young woman in the street, by which she died the following day.

A more serious incident, reminiscent of the Stennack battle in Civil War days, took place in 1729, when the town was attacked by starving Redruth tinners intent on seizing a quantity of corn stored there, probably awaiting shipment. The townsfolk being apprized of possible trouble, had placed the local militia, or watch, in a state of preparedness, and had also secured the services of a number of soldiers. The tinners entered the town via Skidden Hill and St Andrew's Street, but then found their passage barred by armed men lying in wait behind the churchyard wall. Richard Lemyn, their leader, urged his followers on by assuring them that the defenders' guns were only loaded with powder, the design being simply to scare them off. The tinners hung back, doubting that this was so, so he then persuaded them to try to take the town by stratagem, some falling back whilst others infiltrated the place by devious ways, surprising the townsmen in the rear. This plan, however, miscarried, and the defenders' guns, which proved, after all, to be charged with good solid lead, inflicted serious losses on the Redruth men, Lemyn himself apparently being among those killed. The inhabitants of St Ives petitioned Lord Hobart, whose family possessed considerable interest in the town, to obtain redress for their wrongs, the town having been much damaged during the affray. The miners' leaders were induced to sign a paper confessing their misdeeds, begging forgiveness of the St Ives people, and promising not to repeat their offence. The papers relating to this transaction were found among the Hobart muniments at Blickling Hall.

The middle years of the 18th century marked a period of steady growth and prosperity. The Rev Thomas Cox, writing of the place c1714, described it as 'a neat Town for this County. The Inhabitants are wealthy, and have twenty Sail of Ships or more belonging to their Harbour. They drive a great Pilchard-Trade in the Bay.' By 1766 commerce had so further increased that it became necessary to build a new quay.

In 1767, Mr John Knill, Collector of Customs at St Ives, and one of the town's best loved personalities, was elected Mayor. He resumed the practice, discontinued in 1717, of entering up his year's accounts in the Book of Record. There are references to a dinner given to the constables on the Sunday before the Mayor's election; to hiring a cart used for whipping Lanyon, an imposter; to a reward of £5 paid to Saml: and Mr: Daniel for giving information against Joan Richards for selling spirituous liquors 'pursuant to the Mayor's proclamation'; to 6s paid to John Paynter for making the serjeants' cloaks and lacing their hats; to a shilling 'for a pint of beer at six severall houses by way of tasting;' to the purchase of standard weights, scales and measures for the borough at a cost of £15 9s 6d; and a payment to John Nance for painting 46 additional constables' poles for election day—they really must have been expecting trouble! These and other entries show Mr Knill's attachment to the old ceremonies and traditions of the Borough, and his efforts to revitalise municipal affairs.

In 1776, doubtless as a result of the outbreak of the War of American Independence, it was decided to strengthen the defences of St Ives against attack from the sea. Accordingly, by an indenture dated November 7 of that year, the Mayor and Corporation acknowledged receipt from the Right Hon George Lord Viscount Townshend, Master General of His Majesty's Ordnance, of a quantity of guns and ammunition, delivered by the *Endeavour* Sloop, Henry Pennal, master. This *Endeavour* was probably a much smaller vessel than Capt Cook's ship of the same name. She herself was not included in the defences of St Ives, but only her cargo. The store-ships of the Navy were like hoys, with pink sterns, but sloop-rigged. She brought from Woolwich six 9 ft 12-pounders, four $8\frac{1}{2}$ ft 9-pounders, and six $8\frac{1}{2}$ ft 6-pounders, with 'Standing Carriages Compleat with Iron Trucks Stool Bed and Coins'; and 280 round shot for the 12-pounders, 162 for the 9-pounders and 158 for the 6-pounders. From the Tower (of London) came a quantity of ancillary equipment, including ladles with staves, sponges with staves, and runners, wadhooks, and rammers.

In connection with the American War of Independence, a remarkable event occurred at St Ives on February 17, 1780. Davies Gilbert states that during the previous December, a large body of troops had been embarked at New York for the attack on Charlestown, South Carolina; but one of the ships went missing, and was thought, by Sir Harry Clinton, to have borne away for the West Indies. She had on board a detachment of Hessians, who had been forced by the Landgrave of Hesse Cassel to fight on the British side. The vessel in fact nearly reached Charlestown, but damaged by collision with a ship of war during a gale could only sail before the strong westerly wind, which eventually carried it across the Atlantic to St Ives. The ship only carried provisions for a short journey, and although the 250 soldiers arrived safe, they were nearly famished. However, St Ives and the neighbourhood 'contended with each other in efforts, not merely to relieve the distress of these unfortunate persons, but to make them comfortable and happy.' The best lodgings obtainable were provided for the private soldiers, and the officers were daily invited to gentlemen's houses. 'Their sufferings as foreigners on behalf of England had excited general compassion, heightened by the reflection that they were not engaged in maintaining any cause in which their country had an interest, that they were not volunteers, but had been purchased by this nation from an individual entrusted with unlimited power, for the good of a portion of mankind, which he had most basely abused for the sake of private gain, in a manner that must commit his name and memory to infamy, and to the execration of mankind.'

The Napoleonic Wars marked another period of danger for seaports such as St Ives, and its defences were again strengthened. A Volunteer Infantry Regiment, commanded by Lieutenant Colonel James Halse (who later built the mining village of Halsetown, near St Ives) was formed to repel the enemy on land, whilst a body of Sea Fencibles, commanded by Captain Oughten, protected the coastal waters.

These Fencibles saw some active service. On the morning of March 5, 1804 a French lugger privateer captured an English brig about five leagues off St Ives. Capt Oughten immediately ordered two boats to be put off, one commanded by himself, the other by Mr Gyles, the port Surveyor. There being little wind they rowed for the lugger, intending to board her, but as they approached, a breeze sprang up, enabling her to slip her lugs and sail out of reach. However, the Fencibles re-took the brig (the *Morristown*, Capt Harris, from Truro to Swansea with copper ore.) She had six Frenchmen on board and a prizemaster, but Capt. Harris had been put on the privateer. The *Morristown* was sent into Portreath, whilst her French crew were landed at St Ives and marched to Plymouth under a guard of the St Ives Infantry.

Meanwhile the Fencibles rowed to another brig about a league further out, but she observed them, hoisted an English ensign, got up her boarding nettings and fired three broadsides. The Fencibles were obliged to sheer off. Though unsure of her exact identity, they believed her to be a French brig privateer which had captured several coasters off Land's End a month before. The Fencibles returned to St Ives; but about ten that evening they boarded the smuggling schooner *Fly* in the Bay with 244 kegs of spirits and several bags of tobacco on board, the Surveyor effecting the seizure.

The celebrated Revenue Cruiser *Dolphin*, stationed at St Ives, likewise performed the double duty of guarding shipping from attack and chasing smugglers. Greatly daring, she sometimes ventured into enemy waters in pursuit of game, on one occasion (June 1803) engaging a much larger French schooner with 150 men on board off Bordeaux. She also did convoy duty, shepherding merchantmen, for example, from Dublin to Plymouth, and sometimes carried pressed men to their ships. But her principal work lay in combating the activities of the Free Traders, against whom she achieved some notable successes—indeed, a small book could be written about her exploits in this field. She also frequently acted as a lifeboat and salvage vessel, performing several fine rescues, such as that of the *Mary*, dismasted in a gale in Mount's Bay in September 1816 which the *Dolphin* brought safely into St Michael's Mount.

The Napoleonic period was one of great danger for St Ives seamen, and there are still local families who can relate traditions of relatives who were made prisoners or killed at sea by French warships and privateers. On March 28, 1804 the brig *Friendship*, of London (Josias Sincock, master) whilst sailing down the Channel, was seized by a French lugger privateer and carried into Dieppe. On board were three young St Ives apprentices, Thomas Williams, John Tregerthen Short and James Sincock, cousins, and nephews of Capt Sincock. They and the other members of the crew were made prisoners of war. Capt Sincock, and Thomas Cogar, one of the sailors, died in captivity, the others, including twelve-year-old William Sincock, the master's son, were faced with the prospect of ten years' imprisonment in Napoleon's gaols. Thomas Williams escaped no less than four times, and the amazing story of his adventures is related in Sir Edward Hain's 'Prisoners of War in France 1804-1814.' Eventually, after his final recapture, he received Napoleon's pardon, signed by the Emperor himself. Returning to St Ives he became a schoolmaster and parish clerk.

His cousin, J. T. Short, set up a Navigation School at the bottom of Barnoon Hill. He kept a diary from 1817 to 1872 which is a mine of information about local events. In it, for instance, is given a graphic account of the 'Great October' storm of 1823, when many ships were wrecked at St Ives and every particle of sand on Porthminster beach was swept away by the waves. A year later (October 15, 1824) a 'steam vessel' arrived which went into Hayle. Great alarm was occasioned by the appearance of this first steamer on the coast, and boats were manned to go out to her assistance!

On December 9, 1825 a French brig slave-ship, the *Perle*, arrived from St John's, on the coast of Africa, with five negroes on board. The Captain, several officers and five of the crew had died on voyage, and one seaman was buried at St Ives. The negroes were taken on shore by a writ of Habeas Corpus, and forwarded to London, where they were released. The incident aroused great interest locally, and was used by Wilberforce and others to forward the cause of the national Anti-Slavery campaign.

Ten years later (September 29, 1835) Capt J. T. Short recorded that a meeting of the inhabitants had been held in the Town Hall to consider the advisability of lighting the town with gas—'which was approved of by all, with the exception of one man.' The foundation of the gasworks above Porthmeor beach had already been laid on May 19 by Camborne masons, the St Ives masons having demanded one-third more money to carry out the work! The town was illuminated by the new medium on December 21 with a most brilliant light.'

In 1835 the Municipal Reform Act introduced a number of important changes in the running of local affairs. The Corporation was transformed from a self-perpetuating to a democratically elected body, and the office of Recorder abolished. The much-needed reform effectually broke the control which the local squirearchy and other powerful figures had for long exercised over it, though this did not immediately become apparent. For many years past the Corporation had been dominated by James Halse and his friends. At the first democratic election, held on December 26, 1835 Halse's Conservative supporters were faced with a strong Radical challenge, but the ruling party gained a total victory. Halse died in 1838, and was the last to dominate the town in this way.

On June 28, 1838 the coronation of Queen Victoria was celebrated by 600 people sitting down to a dinner on The Terrace at two o'clock, whilst in the evening 800 Wesleyan and Primitive Sunday School children, with several hundred more adults and the aged, were provided with tea there, a band attending through the day. 'At night there were illuminations, when some very good figures were exhibited by gas. The whole finished with an excellent display of fireworks until midnight.'

In February 1841 Capt Short noted: 'On Tuesday last distress warrants were granted for non-payment of gas-rate, when a mob assembled, and insulted and resisted the parish officers; in consequence of which this day at ten o'clock, according to summons, they assembled in the Town Hall, where 120 special constables were sworn in for three months, and the ringleaders in this riotous transaction came forward to the bar and acknowledged in a public court their contrition for their offence, and begged the clemency of the Mayor, and by written and signed documents acknowledged the same.' The county press stated that the authorities were obliged to call in the Coastguard to restore order on this occasion. They afterwards advertised for a London policeman in an effort to restrain further outbreaks of violence against this unpopular rate. In the event, the appointment was secured by James Harvey, of Truro, formerly a private in the Inniskilling Dragoons. He succeeded William Trevorrow, a local man, the first St Ives police officer, appointed on February 10, 1840. The best known policeman here in Victoria times, however, was James Bennetts, who took up his duties on August 9, 1854 at a yearly salary of £35!

On May 8, 1843 a piped water supply was inaugurated, its source being the Tregenna stream, with a small reservoir at Albert Terrace which has recently been converted into a garage. It was paid for by public subscription, Mr Stephens of Tregenna, Mr Praed of Trevetho, and Mr James Richards, formerly a coachman at Trevetho, each contributing £100, and was made available at 'fountains' (standpipes) in various parts of the town.

About sixty young men left St Ives on February 27, 1854 in the *Queen* steamer for Bristol, on their way to Liverpool to embark for Australia. Around this period the diary records a number of wrecks on the Stones, off Godrevy, notably the steamer *Nile* in November 1854. The outcome was the decision to build a lighthouse on Godrevy Island, its light being first exhibited on March 1, 1859.

The first interment in the new Barnoon cemetery took place on March 1, 1857 in the section reserved for Dissenters, the church portion being consecrated by the Bishop of Exeter on May 13. On July 7 the Imperial French screw steamer *La Reine Hortense* anchored in the roadstead to take on board Prince Napoleon, son of Jerome, who, with a retinue, had previously landed at Falmouth to inspect some of the mines between that place and St Ives. Finding no boat had been sent to take him from the quay, the Prince hired an old fishing gig and embarked for the steamer. On leaving, he was accorded three hearty cheers from the assembled crowd which he acknowledged by raising his hat.

On October 25, 1859 the St Ives shipowners suffered grievous losses during the terrible Royal Charter gale, so named after a ship wrecked on Anglesea with the loss of 454 lives, two being from this town. Among the local casualties were the *Sir Robert Peel*, Capt John Richards, lost two miles west of Portreath, all five of her crew being drowned; the *Sultana Selina*, wrecked on the Dunbar at Padstow, seven drowned; and the *John Wesley*, Capt Bryant, believed foundered with her crew. In addition, the *Pearl* of Hayle was lost at St Agnes, and the *Thistle* of the same place, wrecked in Morte Bay, crew saved. The barque *Severn* of Sunderland was lost on Hayle Bar, two of her crew being drowned and one saved. The sloop *Martha Jane* of Plymouth went ashore at Pednolver Point, but the crew were saved. Of six vessels which left Cardiff that morning, bound and belonging to St Ives, only the famous old *Liberty*, skippered by Capt 'Liberty' Andrews, reached port; the other five were lost, so that the town, in Capt Short's own words, was 'full of lamentation and woe.'

Capt J. T. Short died in 1873, and with his passing one might also say that the 'classical' period of St Ives history came to an end, for already the railway that was to break the town's isolation and bring a new way of life to its people was being planned.

In 1647/8 Thomas Noale was Mayor—'I Received of Mr George Hicks
being church warden towards the charge in bringinge down the Organs
Raylinges and other Implements of the Church 18s'—the Puritan influence
at work. (TC; WT)

48

Loving cup and maces with INSET: the inscription on the foot of the cup
(TC; WT), and the town's coat of arms. (M; WT)

ABOVE : Borough Charter, 1685 and BELOW : old Borough seal. (TC; WT)

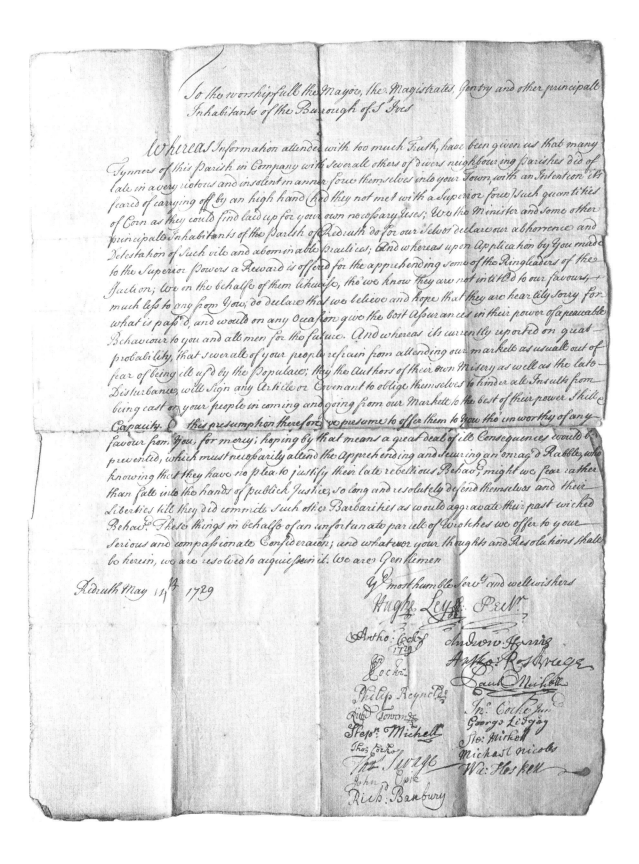

To the worshipfull the Mayor, the Magistrates, Gentry and other principall
Inhabitants of the Burrough of St Ives

Whereas Information attended with too much Truth, have been given us that many
Tynners of this parish in Company with severall others of divers neighbouring parishes did of
late in a very riotous and insolent manner fower themselves into your Town, with an Intention it's
feared of carrying off by an high hand (had they not met with a Superior force) Such quantities
of Corn as they could find laid up for your own necessary Uses; We the Minister and Some other
principall Inhabitants of the parish of Redruth do for our Selves declare our abhorrence and
Detestation of Such vile and abominable practices; And whereas upon Application by You made
to the Superior Powers a Reward is offered for the apprehending some of the Ringleaders of the
faction; we on the behalfe of them likewise, tho' we know they are not intitled to our favours,
much less to any from You; do declare that we believe and hope that they are heartily sorry for
what is pass'd, and would on any Occasion give the best Assurances in their power of a peaceable
Behaviour to you and all men for the future. And whereas it's currently reported on great
probability, that severall of your people refrain from attending our markett as usual out of
fear of being ill us'd by the Populace; they the Authors of their own Misery as well as the late
Disturbance, will Sign any Article or Covenant to oblige themselves to hinder all Insults from
being cast on your people in coming and going from our Markett to the best of their power Skill &
Capacity. On this presumption therefore we presume to offer them to You tho' unworthy of any
favour from You, for mercy; hoping by that means a great deal of ill Consequences would be
prevented, which must necessarily attend the apprehending and Securing an enrag'd Rabble, who
knowing that they have no plea to justify their late rebellious Behav might we fear rather
than fall into the hands of publick Justice, so long and resolutely defend themselves and their
Liberties till they did committ such other Barbarities as would aggravate their past wicked
Behav. These things in behalfe of an unfortunate parcell of Wretches we offer to your
Serious and compassionate Consideration; and whatever your thoughts and Resolutions shall be
be herein, we are resolved to acquiesse in it. We are Gentlemen

Redruth May 14 1729

Yr most humble Servts and wellwishers

Hugh Leigh Pett
Antho: Cock
Coch
Philip Reynolds
Andrew Harris
Antho Rosbridge
Danl Nichott
Jno Coche Jun
George Lidgey
Ste Michell
Thos Coche
Wm Swale
John Opie
Rich: Banbury
Sto: Mirkell
Michael nicoles
Wm Hosken

Tinners' Riot 1729—complaint to the Mayor. (TC & CRO; WT)

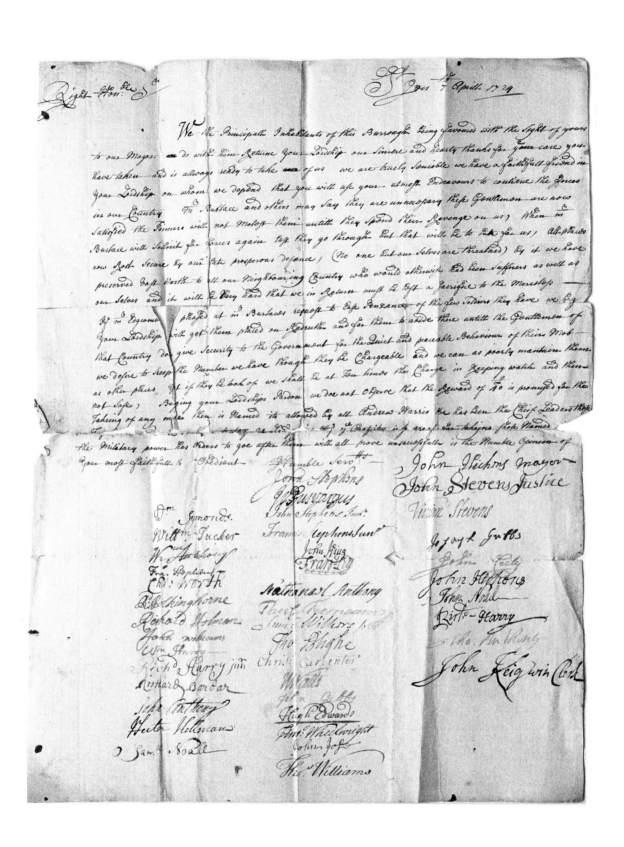

Tinners' Riot 1729—The Corporate response. (TC & CRO; WT)

52

ABOVE: 1745 drawing by Christopher, son of historian Dr William Borlase showing the Carnglaze pier before its 1767 demolition; on the left the old Castle. This is the earliest known picture of the town (PMGL); BELOW: The main road in this 1815 picture once ran hard by Tregenna Castle but was diverted in 1836. (M)

The accounts of Mayor John Knill, 1767/8, entered in his own hand.
(TC; WT)

54

St. IVES BYE LAWS.

—◦✶◦—

BOROUGH OF SAINT IVES.

WE, the Council of the Borough of Saint Ives in the County of Cornwall, being duly convened for that purpose and being upwards of two thirds now present of the whole number of the Council, do hereby, in pursuance and Execution of the powers and authorities enabling us in that behalf under and by Virtue of a certain Act made and passed in the 5th and 6th Years of the Reign of his Majesty, King William the Fourth, entitled " An Act " to provide for the Regulation of Municipal " Corporations in England and Wales," make and publish the following Bye Laws for the good Rule and Government of the said Borough, and for prevention and suppression of all such nuisances and offences as are not already punishable in a summary manner by Virtue of any Law now in force. Sealed with our Seal of the said Borough, this twenty seventh day of January, One thousand, Eight hundred and Thirty seven.

LEFT: Miniature of Betty Wallis, only child and heiress of Capt Samuel Wallis, 18th century explorer; she married Samuel Stephens of Tregenna Castle, and her son Henry Lewis Stephens (1810-67) was the last Squire Stephens of Tregenna (M; WT), RIGHT: 1837 local bye laws (M; WT) and BELOW: from Capt John Tregerthen Short's diary for 1835. (M; WT)

ABOVE LEFT: Berriman family, Treve
RIGHT: Tregenna Castle Hotel (M); CE
former seat of the Praeds and Tyringha
c1830 (WT); RIGHT: Carrack Gladden (
drawing by E. W. Cook
ABOVE RIGHT: Lelant Quay, c1880 (HF
across Hayle River (M), and BELOW :

anor (M; EA);
House, Lelant,
LEFT: St Ives,
cottages, from a

E: Lelant Ferry
ice. (M; EA)

LELANT
POST OFFICE

TELEGRAPH OFFICE

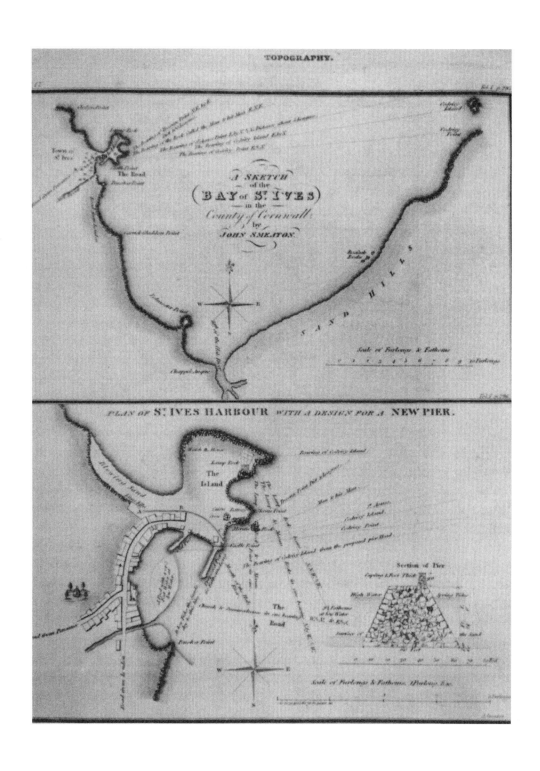

John Smeaton's plan for his new pier.

Peere and Kaye

The harbour is the very centre and focus of activity at St Ives, and has been so through all the centuries back to that distant time when the first fishermen beached their boats here. The construction date of the original quay is unknown. One of the earliest references to a pier occurs in William Worcester's 'Itinerary' (1478) where he gives the distance 'from Penzance to Seynt Yves jette' as '6 myle'—Cornish 'myle,' obviously! By the time of the commencement of the Borough Accounts in 1573 'Quay Wardens' were already numbered among the established parish officers. The quay tolls were farmed out, and the parish, in return, undertook the maintenance of the pier. Thus, in 1576, 10s was 'payd for amending our kaye.' There was already then a thriving seaborne trade at St Ives; so much so that the local businessmen found their interests were injured by it; in 1580 a by-law was enacted forbidding any 'forestman' (stranger) to land 'apples, peson (peas) or malte' within eight days of arriving within the quay, whilst townsmen were not to 'sett any seller vnto any one of them' within fifteen days, subject to a penalty of 10s.

In 1581 the State Papers Domestic refer to a petition of certain Justices of Cornwall to the Privy Council 'on behalf of the town of St Tyes' for the renewal of patents for erecting a new pier there, and to make collections for that purpose. This seems to imply that the old pier was past repair or perhaps had been washed down in a storm.

The parish was certainly unremitting in its efforts to improve the harbour. In 1592 the authorities 'bestowed in drincke upon the tynners ffor digginge up the stones with in the kay 1s 10d.' In 1595 they 'paid for mendinge of the koine (coign) of the keaye 8s 6d.' A regulation was enacted in 1619 'requiring all ships & Barcks' with a 'Top' taking on sand or ballast to pay 2s, or without a 'Top' 6d, whilst strangers laying hogsheads of fish or lime on the pier must pay 2d per ton.

New harbour dues were introduced in 1626 to pay for the repair of the 'Peere or Kaye' of St Ives which had become much decayed, 'the postes wasted and the sandes much annoyeing aboute the porth and the houses and sellers adioyninge.'

In 1658 a payment of 1s 6d was recorded for 'cappinge the poste on the keye head,' whilst in 1671 £1 1s was paid for '10 c waight of plaister of pallace (plaster of Paris) for the head of the Key and for carriadge.' The old 'keye' thus being constantly repaired ran off from under Carn Glaze. What, then, should one make of this singular entry in 1695: 'paid to amend the chapell on the kay 16s 10d.'? There certainly was no chapel on the Carn Glaze quay, but St Leonard's chapel is to be found at the entrance to the present Smeaton's Pier, on the Castle Rock. Could there have been a small quay or jetty there in 1695, or was the term 'quay' applied somewhat loosely to the entire harbour frontage at that time?

The considerable increase in the fishing and mercantile fleets of the port during the 18th century made improved harbour facilities imperative, and in 1766, at the instigation of John Knill, the great engineer John Smeaton was invited to St Ives to advise what should be done to achieve this object. Smeaton carried out a considerable amount of work in Cornwall, making plans for harbour improvements, surveying a canal, and reporting on the performance of pumping engines in the mines. His greatest achievement, however, was the construction of the third Eddystone lighthouse in 1759, which has since been rebuilt on the Hoe at Plymouth.

In his report on St Ives, Smeaton stated: 'At the north-west corner of this bay a bold, rocky promontory, called the *Island*, is joined by a narrow neck to the mainland, and projecting considerably forwards towards the east, forms a natural harbour on the north-west side of the bay, and defended from all winds except the north-easterly. This interior bay forms the harbour of *St Ives*, and is for the most part left dry at low spring tides; but on account of the fine, soft sand . . . that universally lines the whole bottom of the bay, affords a soft, easy bed for ships to lay upon when left by the tides; and for such ships as have not occasion, cannot, or choose not, to come upon ground, here is an excellent road where ships of every burthen may ride, safe from all north-westerly, westerly, south-westerly, southerly and south-easterly winds, in six and seven fathoms of water, at low water spring tides.'

With a north or north-easterly gale, however, the bay became a death-trap for ships, which consequently avoided it, only, in many cases, to be cast ashore on other parts of the north Cornish coast, there being no harbour of safety within 28 leagues. Smeaton therefore proposed to construct a breakwater from Castle Point 60 fathoms long in a southerly direction, which would afford shelter for about 60 sail in all winds. There should seldom be less than 20 ft of water round the pier head at high water, and never less than 18; whilst the set of the tides would enable any vessel riding in the roadstead to slip her cable, if hard pressed, and sail within the pier, whenever there was water there.

Foreseeing the possibility that the harbour might be choked by the sand which blew from Porthmeor over the peninsula, almost burying the houses there, he recommended building a wall 25-30 ft high to deflect the wind-borne sand to the north of Castle Point. His advice, in this particular, was not followed till 1801, and the wall then built (at a cost of £270) ran across the back of Porthmeor Beach between the northern end of the Digey and the western side of the Island; it proved completely effective, stabilising the sand bank, and enabling houses to be built on all parts of the isthmus.

The method Smeaton recommended for constructing the breakwater was to lay rough stones on top of the sand, which would pack hard and form a sufficient foundation, known to the French as *pierre perdue*. He proposed continuing the pier according to these principles up to half-tide, or even to the top, which meant it would have an appreciable batter on both sides, as shown in the cross-section, arguing that as the structure was intended principally as a breakwater, the lack of uprightness on the inside for the purposes of a quay was of little consequence. In the event, however, the structure was built with vertical sides, the authorities doubtless deciding that it should be made to serve a double purpose, in view of the great outlay involved. Had his plan been followed, the pier would have risen to a height of 36 ft, bringing it (with allowance for settlement) to 4 ft above high springs, and had a base width of 60 ft with a top width of 24 ft. His recommendation that a protective parapet be placed on the outer side was adopted.

Construction began in 1767, and was completed three years later. Mr Thomas Richardson, a mason who had assisted Smeaton in making his survey, was the contractor. The total cost of the pier and wharves (including the Wharf between Quay Street and Chy-an-Chy) came to £9,477 8s 8d, as against Smeaton's estimate of £7,985, the difference probably arising from the extra cost of building the breakwater as a quay. Due to the lack of suitable roads, all the stone required was conveyed in boats from Zennor cliffs—no easy task.

In 1798 an adit was driven through the Castle Rock, and a reservoir and launders built to flush sand from the harbour, in accordance with one of Smeaton's recommendations. Between 1805-7 no less than £1,193 15s 10d was paid for 'blasting rocks and removing them from the pier,' whilst in 1811 Capt Richard Trevithick, the famous Cornish engineer, received £82 2s for surveying an outer breakwater to form an intended harbour of refuge. Francis Jenkyns, of St Ives, also acted as a surveyor to this scheme.

The work was to have extended 2,000 ft or more in an easterly direction from Merran Rock, off Porthgwidden, and been provided with a harbour light. However, due to the objection of shipping interests to the higher dues necessary to pay for it, the plan was dropped. A more modest scheme was brought forward in 1815 for a protective breakwater at the back of Smeaton's Pier, for which Samuel Moyle, of Truro, was appointed engineer.

The stone-laying ceremony took place on April 10, 1817, the event marked by a procession consisting of 'The Band and Colours of the late Regiment of the St Ives Volunteers; the Mayor, Recorder, Aldermen of the Borough and County Magistrates (Trustees of the Pier); the most respectable Inhabitants of St Ives and its neighbourhood; followed by an immense concourse of Mechanics and Labourers.' This 'foundation stone' consisted of a large rock weighing six tons; suspended from a crane, it was lowered to a tram waggon which the Mayor, Recorder and Magistrates pushed to the end of the tramroad, when 'it was instantly immerged into the sea, amidst the roar of cannon (from a beautiful battery of sixteen 18-pounders) and the acclamation of the numerous spectators. . . . Afterwards the Gentlemen returned to the Star Inn, where they partook of an elegant dinner, and the day was spent with the greatest harmony and conviviality.'

When Capt James Vetch, RN, published a Report on St Ives Harbour in 1847, he stated that though 16,506 tons of stone had been deposited in the sea, he could perceive no vestige of the 1817 breakwater then remaining. This was probably because he looked in the wrong place, for it is impossible to believe that six-ton rocks could have completely disappeared during the interim. In actual fact, much of the work still survives in the form of an immense disintegrated bank of rocks extending seawards from Bamaluz Point.

In 1824 an ambitious Harbour of Refuge scheme was mooted, but proved abortive. A picturesque stone lighthouse was built on the end of Smeaton's Pier in 1831 at a cost of £238 16s, the architects being James and Edward Harvey. Prior to this, the quayhead light had consisted of a lantern on a pole. Under the 1766 St Ives Pier Act the management of the harbour had been vested in a body of trustees, comprising the County and Borough Magistrates. They derived their income from dues on fish and merchandise; but in 1837 these were abolished, despite local opposition, and the harbour declared a free port.

The ever-increasing growth of the trade and fishery of St Ives soon after this began to cause inconvenience. The old harbour was now too small, and so in 1853 a new Act was obtained for erecting an additional pier 400 ft long, but this lapsed in 1861 without further progress. In 1862 an Order was obtained for building a pier of 600 ft to run off from Castle Rock in an easterly direction, forming an outer harbour. Work on this project commenced in 1864, and dues were reimposed to recover the cost. The old 1798 adit was closed up again at the same time.

This—the 'New Pier,' as it came to be known—proved a dismal failure. Consisting for the greater part of its length of a wooden framework filled with loose stones, it soon disintegrated under the battering of the north-easterly gales; its position is marked today only by its short masonry base and a line of stones with a few broken piles extending seawards.

The destruction of this pier proved a disaster for the fishermen; and in 1888, following the grant of a new Order, work was begun on an extension to Smeaton's Pier, which about doubled the size of the harbour. This addition, known as the Victoria Extension, was 280 ft long, making the total length of the quay 600 ft. It broadened considerably around the junction with the original structure, but on the outer side a concave sweep of 100 ft brought the 66 ft width of Smeaton's Pier to a width of 35 ft, which was continued to the end. Here a cast-iron lighthouse made by Messrs Stothert & Pitt Ltd, of Bath was erected.

A total of 450 piles was driven into the sand to obtain a good foundation, and the spaces between filled with Portland cement. Upon this 'grid' was raised the 'core' of the pier, consisting of concrete blocks, the exterior being faced with Cornish granite.

At the same time three curious stone arches were pierced through the base of Smeaton's Pier as a means of relieving the harbour of its old enemy, the sand, but they proved altogether too effective, boats being sucked through them as well by the receding tide, and they were soon blocked again with wooden baulks.

The foundation stone of the Victoria Extension was laid on June 25, 1888, by T. B. Bolitho, and the final stone by Mr (later Sir) Edward Hain exactly two years later. William Matthews, CE, held the position of engineer to the undertaking, and the contractors were Messrs Lang & Son. The total cost was £19,162.

The last important addition to the harbour at St Ives was completed in 1894, when the West Pier, running off by the lifeboat house, came into use for shipping off roadstone from Carthew Quarry. Its principal features are a hand-worked crane and an ornamental blue lamp.

Sir Edward Hain, founder of the Hain Steamship Company, was born at St Ives in 1851. 'Hain' appears in the Borough records in Elizabethan times. During the mid-nineteenth century Sir Edward's father, Capt Edward Hain, built up a small fleet of merchant sailing vessels—the *Camilla*, *Mystery*, *Glynn*, *Margaret Hain*, *Bohemian Girl* and others. In 1878 Edward pursuaded his somewhat reluctant father to make the transition from sail to steam; their first steamer, named the *Trewidden*, was commissioned that year, and a large number followed in quick succession, all bearing Cornish place names with the prefix *Tre*. For many years all Hain ships were built at Shields by John Readhead and Sons, an association probably unique in British shipbuilding.

Sir Edward was elected MP for St Ives in 1900, and in 1910 became President of the Chamber of Shipping, and received his knighthood. In 1911 he received the Freedom of the Borough of St Ives, of which he had previously been six times Mayor. He was elected Sheriff of Cornwall in 1912, and at the outbreak of war in 1914 was appointed by the Board of Trade to sit on the Committee on Shipping and Ship Building.

Sir Edward's only son, Capt Edward Hain, was killed at Gallipoli in 1915; this hastened Sir Edward's own death in 1917. Soon afterwards the Hain Steamship Company was acquired by the P & O group, and its office transferred in 1925 to London.

The Hain fleet served in both World Wars, with grievous losses in men and ships. In recent years, the trend towards large bulk carriers led to a decision by the controlling Company to phase out the Hain line.

THE COMMISSIONERS of the ST. IVES NEW PIER ACT will please Take Notice, that it is the intention of the Inhabitants of this Town to have a NEW PIER.

DEAR FELLOW-TOWNSMEN,

I beg to present to you for your consideration the following Sections of the ST. IVES NEW PIER ACT, which received the Royal Assent, 4th August, 1853:—

XXX.—"That the powers of the Commissioners for the compulsory purchase of lands for the purposes of this Act shall not be exercised "after the expiration of Five Years from the passing of this Act."

XXXI.—"That the intended Pier shall be completed within SEVEN Years from the passing of this Act, and on the expiration of that "period the powers by this Act and the Acts incorporated herewith given to the Commissioners with reference to the intended Pier "shall cease to be exercised, except as to so much of the same Pier as shall then be completed."

This Act cost nearly £2000, and not an *earnest* effort has been made on the part of its promoters to carry it out. Four years are already wasted: 4 out of 7 for the building of the Pier, and 4 out of 5 for the compulsory purchase of lands.

The Money is wanting!! We all know this, and it will NEVER be raised in St. Ives in good or bad times; and, we are all pretty well tired of trusting to Members of Parliament. Still, *can we not do something for ourselves?* If we are not wealthy, we can do, what many rich men do, borrow on good security: only get an Act with powers to levy a Borough Rate, and you would find money lenders very gracious.

Who would not sign a Petition to Government, praying for its support in getting an Amended Act, to empower the CORPORATION to make Rates to meet any deficiences that might arise in the working of the Pier? and to let that old and respected body have its entire management? what need of two bodies? a thousand signatures would be affixed to such a Petition in a week. Fishermen are interested in a New Pier for the sake of their immense property; and we are all Fishermen in St. Ives,—Ship-owners, for the sake of their ships,—Tradesmen, for the sake of their well-stocked shops, without buyers,—Sailors, and the community at large, for the sake of their lives: in fact, there is not a Labouring Man a-mongst us who would not be benefitted by it. Who says that Government will not grant such power in an Act? no one *knows* it. What objection is there to send a Petition? Government Agents have visited us often, and reports have been printed, all acknowledging that a Harbour is much wanted. If we can show by our unanimity that we are of one mind, and further, that we can build the Pier ourselves only enable us to give legal security for the money, I believe they would grant us what we ask.

The Pier has from the beginning been sacrificed to the interests and ambition of the *few.* Who are most frightened at the sound of "more rates"? *only the few.* A PUBLIC MEETING for the voice of the *many!!* Why shall we not send a Petition and try? *NO PIER, NO PROSPERITY!!!*

I am, Dear Fellow-Townsmen,
Your most obedient Servant,

A ST. IVES-MAN, BORN & BRED.

W. KERNICK, Printer, Bookseller, Stationer, &c., Tregenna Place, ST. IVES.

Poster appealing for a new pier, *c*1857. (M; WT)

ABOVE: The Harbour c1850 (RIC); LEFT: announcing the foundation
stone laying ceremony for the New Pier, 1864 (M; WT); RIGHT: laying the
stone—for the wooden pier, August 30, 1864. (M; My)
INSET: John Smeaton. (M)

ABOVE: Wood Pier under construction July 1866 (HF; EA); CENTRE:
Beer dray at the White Hart Hotel on the Wharf, c1870 (M) and BELOW:
Smeaton's Pier, c1880. (EA)

ABOVE: Laying the foundation stone of the Victoria Extension to Smeaton's
Pier, 1888 (SSI) and BELOW: the Pier prior to the extension. The ruined
Wood Pier is in the background. (RIC; EA)

LEFT: Smeaton's Pier extension completion, 1890 (SSI); RIGHT: Wharf Road was later built here, and BELOW: the West Pier nearing completion in 1894. (EA)

ABOVE: The Harbour in 1900 (M); LEFT: schooner *Ulelia* (built at Sunny Corner) unloading coal on the beach (RIC; EA) and RIGHT: Godrevy Lighthouse *c*1900. (M; JCD)

ABOVE: The *Margaret Hain* of St Ives (M); CENTRE: ss *Trelyon* of the
Hain fleet; LEFT: Lady Hain (with parasol) on the Wharf (SSI) and Sir
Edward Hain (1851-1917), founder of the Hain Steamship Company. (SSI)

ABOVE : A fishing boat takes shape in the harbour (PQ); BELOW : Paynter's
boatbuilding yard, now Woolworths. (M)

ABOVE: Boatbuilding in the harbour; LEFT: J. R. Cothey, one of the last
St Ives boatbuilders (SB); RIGHT: Thomas Thomas, boatbuilder of
Wharf Road. (M)

ABOVE: Lifeboat launch in the harbour, *c*1880; CENTRE: ss *Rosedale* wrecked at Porthminster November 17, 1893 (RIC); BELOW: schooners *Lizzie R. Wilce* of Falmouth and *Mary Barrow* of Barrow also wrecked at Porthminster, January 7 and 8, 1908 (RIC); RIGHT: schooner *Susan Elizabeth*—same fate, same place, October 17, 1907. (M)

The Lifesavers

The first St Ives lifeboat was the *Hope*, designed and built in 1840 by Francis Jennings Adams, a local boatbuilder. The RNLI established a station here in 1860 and forwarded the lifeboat *Moses* to St Ives the following year; she was kept in a house near the Island. Her most famous service occurred on October 28, 1865, when she twice capsized in a terrible storm when going to the assistance of the brig *Providence* of Granville, wrecked on Hayle Bar. Four sailors were rescued, and Coxswain Levett received a silver medal for his heroism.

Her successor (in 1866) was the *Moses II*, later re-named *Covent Garden* and *Exeter*. The present lifeboat house at Market Strand was built for her a year later. Her coxswains included two celebrated lifeboatmen, Paul Curnow and James Murphy, who between them carried out many gallant services. On February 2, 1873 the *Covent Garden* was launched no less than five times to save the crews of three vessels wrecked in a severe storm, the schooners *Mary Ann* and *Rambler* of Plymouth and brig *Frances* of Porthcawl. Two silver medals were awarded on this occasion.

A second *Exeter* arrived in 1886. Then, in 1900, St Ives' most famous rowing lifeboat, the *James Stevens No 10*, came on station and remained here 33 years, during which time she saved the magnificent total of 227 lives, some made under difficult wartime conditions. Among her coxswains were Thomas Quick, Thomas Stevens and Robert Wedge.

St Ives' first motor lifeboat, the *Caroline Parsons*, appeared in 1933, but on January 31, 1938 she was wrecked on the Island whilst rescuing the crew of the ss *Alba* of Panama. Coxswain Thomas Cocking received a silver medal and the crew bronze medals for this service, whilst the Hungarian Government presented a Gold Cross of Merit to the Coxswain and a similar award to the Mayor (C. W. Curnow) in recognition of the gallantry and courage displayed by the townsfolk.

A second lifeboat disaster occurred about a year later, on January 23, 1939, when the *John and Sarah Eliza Stych* launched to the assistance of a ship thought to be the ss *Wilston* of Glasgow, wrecked under Tregerthen cliffs. She capsized three times in the heavy seas, seven out of the eight members of her crew being swept away and drowned, and was finally cast ashore at Gwithian, the sole survivor of that terrible night being William Freeman, a volunteer.

This tragedy resulted in the temporary closing of the station, but it reopened in 1940, soon after launching by tractor instead of by hand. Since then a succession of lifeboats has given unstinted service both in war and peace. Coxswains during this period have included William Peters, Daniel Roach and Thomas Cocking. The present lifeboat is the *Frank Penfold Marshall*, of the 37 ft Oakley type; the lifeboat house had to be practically rebuilt in 1969 to accommodate her. In 1976 she was equipped with radar, the first lifeboat of her type to be provided with this facility. The work of the station has been greatly assisted in recent years by the presence of a small inshore rescue boat, whose speed and manoeuvrability have proved invaluable for rescuing bathers in difficulties and for similar duties.

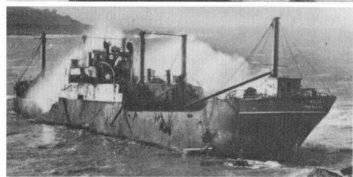

ABOVE: Launching the lifeboat by hand (DP); CENTRE: the lifeboat slip-
way before Wharf Road was built in 1922 (SSI); LEFT: ss *Alba* wrecked
January 31, 1938; RIGHT: ketch *Cicelia* wrecked at Pednolver Point after
drifting from her Smeaton Pier moorings January 1935—the last sailing
ship wrecked at St Ives (SSI); BELOW: the St Ives lifeboat *John and Sarah
Eliza Stych* wrecked at Gwithian, January 1939. (SSI)

Hevva!

Surveying the gay summertime scene in St Ives harbour today, with brightly coloured pleasure craft of all descriptions bobbing on the sparkling water and children playing on the beach, it is difficult to believe that just eighty years ago, in 1896, this place ranked as fourth among the English ports for the quantity of fish landed, and that laden fish carts arriving at the station were not infrequently turned away, the railway company being unable to accept all the traffic offered them.

The fishermen's year at St Ives was divided into a number of distinct seasons. The first, starting soon after 'Feast' in February, was the mackerel drift fishery. The large mackerel luggers which had been laid up at Lelant during the winter, would be overhauled and taken to St Ives to be equipped with nets and gear. Fishing was carried out some distance from land in the Channel, and later (from April to June) near the Scilly Isles. The men took several days' provisions with them and often sent their catches back to shore in a boat chosen for this purpose, whilst they continued fishing without interruption. From the 1860's onwards small steamers plied between the Scilly fishing grounds and Penzance to bring the mackerel ashore quickly and in good condition.

The summer was devoted to crabbing, crayfish and lobsters also being caught in the nets and baited 'pots' usually placed in sheltered bays or near reefs where these creatures congregated. With the end of the mackerel fishery around midsummer, a number of the large mackerel boats prepared to go to the North Sea to take part in the herring fishery there. Sailing up the Welsh and English coast to Scotland, they passed through the Caledonian Canal and then began to follow the herring shoals down the east coast, basing themselves in turn on Berwick, Whitby, Scarborough, Yarmouth and Lowestoft, sailing home along the south coast. The arrival of the boats in September was eagerly awaited, and the men usually brought presents for their wives and children—nests of brown pottery Whitby pans, sticks of Scarborough rock, and—sometimes—bottles of perfume and roll tobacco purchased duty-free on the high seas from Dutch 'coopers.' The Customs authorities were well aware of this and occasionally rummaged the boats as they came in.

Some boats also participated in the Irish summer herring fishery. This was started in the year 1816 by a St Ives fisherman called Noall, and the bold attempt succeeded. At first only two or three engaged in it; the next year the number increased to twelve, and before long they were joined by boats from Newlyn and Mousehole. The first boats to go to Ireland from St Ives were small half-decked luggers, providing scant shelter and little comfort for their crews.

The late summer and autumn (August to November) was the pilchard season. These fish were taken in two different ways—by the pilchard drivers, a smaller class of lugger than the mackerel boats, and by seining. The drivers operated both in St Ives Bay and 'around land' at Newlyn and Mousehole. Seining was an entirely distinct fishery, and pursued in a manner quite different from any other. It depended on the habit of pilchard shoals—sometimes numbering hundreds of millions of fish—frequenting the sandy coves and bays around the Cornish coast. This enabled them to be trapped in huge seine nets, each a quarter of a mile long, which were shot around the pilchards in a circle and the ends closed by a stop-net, the seine then being drawn close to shore by warps attached to capstans on the beach. The footline of the net was weighted with leads and the top buoyed with corks, so that the fish were trapped alive in a mesh prison. They could then be removed from the seine at leisure by small tuck nets, and after being ferried to the harbour in boats known as 'dippers' were dry cured in salt, or 'bulked,' pressed to extract the oil and brine, and shipped in large casks, called hogsheads, to Italy, where there was a large demand for them, particularly during Lent.

Seining required the outlay of large sums of money on labour, boats, nets, cellars, salt and casks, and so was run on capitalist lines by a number of big companies. (By contrast, the other local fisheries operated on a 'share' basis, the men, boats and nets all receiving their appropriate portions.) Seining was highly organised and regulated, at first, in the 16th and 17th centuries, according to by-laws enacted by the local council, and later by two Acts of Parliament dated 1776 and 1841. It was also an extremely colourful and picturesque industry. When the watching 'huers' at the baulking house on Porthminster Point sighted a shoal, they at once alerted the town by shouting 'Hevva!' through their long speaking trumpets; and then, with a complicated series of signals given by their white 'bushes' or semaphores, directed the waiting seine boats at stem how best to shoot their net to enclose the fish. It was a truly wonderful spectacle, but one which will never be seen again, as this fishery died out just after the first World War.

October saw the start of the herring season, which lasted until Christmas. St Ives herrings had the reputation of being the finest flavoured that could be caught anywhere, but the men who went after them ran great risks, owing to the autumn gales, and to the fact that the best catches were often made in the most dangerous places, such as near the Stones, off Godrevy.

Apart from these main fisheries, there were others of lesser importance—small tackling in sandy bays for plaice, dabs, flukes, turbot, brill, whiting, gurnets and rays, and line-fishing for bream, chads, gurnets and scads (horse mackerel.) Trawling, blind-hauling and long-lining were also carried on; and even the despised and detested hake and dogfish were at one time keenly pursued, the latter being despatched to London under the more acceptable name of 'rock salmon.'

It is an interesting fact that St Ives owed its valuable drift fisheries to Breton fishermen who regularly crossed the Channel to fish in local waters. When Louis XIV revoked the Edict of Nantes in 1685, Huguenot refugees settled at St Ives. Bitter quarrels occurred between these people and the Catholic Bretons who stored their fishing gear in a barn-like building on the southern side of the Island known as the 'Breton's hut,' only a few fragments of which now remain. Porthgwidden Cove was then the principal landing place for St Ives fishing boats; and it is said that the first knowledge the local men had of the drift fishery was their finding on Porthgwidden beach some Frenchmen's nets with mackerel enmeshed in them, following an encounter between the Huguenots and Bretons in which the latter were worsted.

Fishing gave rise to a number of important subsidiary industries, chief among them boat-building. During the last century many boats were built here not only for the local fishermen but for Cornwall generally, the Isle of Man, Ireland, Lowestoft and other east coast ports, whilst boatbuilders elsewhere copied the St Ives models—a striking testimony to their sea-worthy qualities. Among the better known boatbuilders were Robert Bryant, who built the *Mary Catherine* and *Jonadab* in his yard near the Island in 1882; T. Hambly, builder of the *Hugh Bourne*, 1882; William Williams, who built the *James*, 1882, *Uncle Tom* and *Boy Tom*, 1883, and *Silvery Light*, 1884, on the Fore Sand; and H. Trevorrow, builder of the *Water Lily*, 1882, and *Young John*, 1883. William Paynter, N. Congdon and J. T. Short also owned boatbuilding yards in the harbour where many fine luggers first saw the light of day. William Williams' *Silvery Light* was an exceptionally fine craft; with an overall length of 75.81 ft, she was built of English oak for W. Chard, of Yarmouth, being intended for the deep-sea herring fishery. The *Uncle Tom*, with a keel of 52.5 ft, and planked with $1\frac{3}{4}$ inch pitchpine, was one of the largest luggers ever built here, being launched from a cradle instead of the more conventional wheels.

The vast quantities of herrings landed at St Ives towards the close of last century led to a curing industry being established for making kippers, bloaters and red herrings. W. Rounce-field's business commenced in 1894, and other smoke houses were opened soon after, all situated near the Island. Nimble-fingered Scotch girls were employed to prepare the fish for curing.

Numbers of coopers were engaged in making the hogsheads required for exporting pil-chards. Isaac England ran a busy net-making factory opposite the Bible Christian chapel in Back Roads, whilst there were ropewalks at the Ropewalk, Park-an-Roper ('the roper's field'), Halsetown and the Warren. Sailmakers were kept busy making the brown lugsails that formed so characteristic a feature of the fishing luggers.

The St Ives fisheries generally were at their peak between 1860 and 1900, their develop-ment stimulated by the opening of through railway communication between Penzance and London in 1859, which enabled vast new markets to be reached. Seine fishing began to decline in the 1880's, and after 1900 fewer mackerel were landed, possibly through over-fishing. The introduction of steam and then oil engines (around 1910) offered no permanent solution to the problems with which the industry was beset, and the fleet sank to insignificant pro-portions during the inter-War years. Recently there has been a modest but significant revival, and it is to be hoped that fishing will one day resume something of its traditional role in the economy and life of St Ives.

Seine net shot off Porthminster Beach. (RIC)

The 16th day of September 1736 (14)

Seine fishery by-law 1736. (TC; WT)

ABOVE: An extremely rare early photo of seine fishermen in their boat
with the 'tilt' spread (HF; EA); BELOW: Porthminster and Primrose
Valley before the railway came. (PQ)

LEFT: Huer signalling with 'bushes' at the Porthminster Baulking House (M); RIGHT: warping in a seine at Porthminster beach (LEC) and BELOW: repairing a seine net. (PQ)

ABOVE: Bathers and seine boats (PQ); CENTRE: Porthminster stemming list August–October 1864—successful enclosures are noted in the last column of the left-hand page in hogsheads (hhd) of some 3,000 fish (M; WT); BELOW: end of the seiners—the last five boats registered in 1920. (M; WT)

An Act for the Encouragement and Improvement of the Pilchard-fishery carried on within the Bay of *Saint Ives*, in the County of *Cornwall*.

ᵂᴴᴱᴿᴱᴬˢ a Pilchard-fishery hath for Preamble. many Years been carried on in the Bay of Saint Ives, in the County of Cornwall, and the carrying on and Improvement thereof is of great Importance to this Nation, by increasing the Trade and Navigation thereof, and being a Nursery for Seamen, and otherwise a Means of employing and providing for a Number of industrious poor People: And whereas the said Fishery hath hitherto been conducted and carried on according to, and regulated by, certain Customs or Regulations which have from Time to Time been devised by the Fishermen and Fishcurers concerned and employed in the said Fishery, which by mutual Consent have been

11 M 2   observed

LEFT: St Ives Pilchard Fishery Act of 1776 (WT); RIGHT: tucking pilchards (RIC) and BELOW: bulking (dry salting) pilchards in Maid Betsey's Cellar (now Barnaloft Flats) in the great pilchard season of 1871. (M)

ABOVE: Fish barrels and baskets on the Wharf, near the bottom of Fish Street (LEC); BELOW: packing fish near the Sloop Inn. (RIC)

83

Boundaries of the Stems ascertained.

II. And be it enacted, That the Six several Stems or Stations for taking Fish within the said Bay of *Saint Ives*, respectively called or known by the Names of *Carrick Gladden*, the *Poll*, the *Leigh*, *Porthminster*, *Pedn Olver*, and *Carrick Leggoe* otherwise *Carn Crowze* Stems, shall from and after the passing of this Act be deemed and taken to be bounded and limited in manner herein-after particularly mentioned; that is to say, the *Carrick Gladden* Stem is to be unlimited towards the South and towards the East, and to extend towards the North as far as the Marks or Boundaries set up and erected in *Porth Repta* River, in pursuance of the said recited Act; the *Poll* Stem is to extend towards the North from the said Marks or Boundaries in *Porth Repta* River, as far as the Marks or Boundaries set up and erected on the North Side of a certain Hedge or Fence, being the Fourth Fence from a House called the *Signal House*, on *Porthminster Hill*, to the Southward of the said House; the *Leigh* Stem is to extend towards the North from the End of the *Poll* Stem, according to the Boundary herein-before mentioned, as far as the *Carrick Rock* opposite *Porthminster Point*; the *Porthminster* Stem is to extend towards the North from the said *Carrick Rock* as far as the Marks or Boundaries which are set up and erected on the Banks of the *Porthminster* River; and the *Pedn Olver* Stem is to extend towards the North from the said Marks or Boundaries on the Banks of the *Porthminster* River as far as the Marks or Boundaries already set up near the present South Corner of the Churchyard in the said Town of *Saint Ives*; and the *Carrick Leggoe* or *Carn Crowze* Stem is to extend towards the South as far as the Marks or Boundaries so set up near the said present South Corner of the said Churchyard, and to be unlimited towards the North.

ABOVE: Stem boundaries described in the 1841 St Ives Pilchard Fishery Act (M; WT) and BELOW: cleaning ling in the 1870's. (M; FF)

ABOVE: Skinning dogfish opposite the Sloop Inn (SSI) and BELOW:
conger sale on the beach with William Veal (merchant), 'Maffo Dukes'
Stevens, 'Har Charles' Paynter and Charles Lander.

85

ABOVE: Jack the Ferry's house crouches by the waterside as luggers sail
along Lelant River (SSI) and BELOW: Capt Lewis Gyles aboard ship.
(M; FF)

ABOVE: ss 502 *Prince* rests in the harbour, *c*1880 (RIC; EA) and BELOW:
a decade later the harbour is crowded with seine boats, fishing vessels, a
schooner and fish carts. (HF; EA)

ABOVE LEFT: ss 120 *Mary Lizzie* (EA) and BE
in the 1880's, while CENTRE: men load gurr
RIGHT: the catch goes by cart (HF) while BEL
and stare along the harbour from the Custom H
was built. (M)

at ease
ABOVE
stand
Road

ABOVE: St Ives lugger ss 583 *Cogar* (M; JCD); and BELOW: Barking (dipping in cutch) to preserve and dye nets at the Bark-house on the Island. (RIC; EA)

Two groups of fishermen. (M)

LEFT: Joanies, often carved from old 'sweeps' (large oars) (M; WT);
RIGHT: George Quick, Methodist lay preacher, boat owner and Bay
fisherman despite his limp. (M)

Hard to Come By

Although fishing held pride of place as the principal industry at St Ives, there was a time, particularly during the early and mid-19th century, when mining came a challenging second, whilst in the neighbouring parishes of Lelant and Towednack, it equalled and possibly surpassed agriculture in economic importance. Mining was also an ancient occupation in this district. The old name of 'Stennack' given to the valley which runs down to the town from the western hills means 'place of tin,' and indicates that tin streaming and mining were carried on here centuries ago when Cornish was still the commonly spoken language. Nor was tin the only metal exploited in those early times, as shown by correspondence preserved among the State Papers. On July 5, 1585 Ulricke Frose wrote from Neath to Robert Denham in Cornwall requesting a further supply of copper ore, 'for they have found out a way to melt 24 cwt of ore per day in one furnace, the Lord be thankful,' adding that the ores of St Ives were very hard, but what those of 'St Ust' (St Just) would be they longed to see. On October 25 of the same year John Otes informed William Carnsewe that he had been at St Ives with letters relating to the shipment of copper ore for Wales. He had received a freight of timber from Wales, but there was no ore ready to be shipped in return. 'A constant supply of ore must be kept at St Ives during the summer.' Money was also required for paying the workmen.

Standing boldly on the coastal plain east of Treveal valley may be seen the stamps engine house of Trevegia Bal, one of the oldest mines in the district, which was started by Matthew Oates, of Ludgvan, in 1674. Around the year 1700 the new method of blasting rocks by powder was first introduced into West Cornwall at this mine by two men called Bell and Care who had learned it from some Germans in the eastern part of the county. They allowed no one to see them charge the holes, but a Zennor man, more cunning than his comrades, hid himself while they were at work and so discovered their secret.

This revolutionary technique enabled deep mining to make much more rapid progress, and during the 18th century several mines were started in the St Ives district which were destined to develop into fairly large concerns. One of the earliest of these seems to have been Wheal Margery, whose workings extend from the National Trust cliffs south-east of Porthminster Point through Treloyhan Manor grounds into Tregenna park. This mine was mentioned in a report drawn up in 1782 by John Knill and others concerning a proposed new road which was to run 'from the corner of Mr Anthony's Cellar upon the Beach, & on through the Warren, & through the Ground beyond the new Stamping Mill so as to come out into the present Road a small distance to the Northward of Wheal Margery Mine.' It developed into a submarine mine, some of its levels being driven a short distance out under the Bay. Operations finally ceased here in 1868, following a boiler explosion in which Abraham Craze, an engineman, was fatally injured.

Wheal Providence, at Carbis Bay, whose sett ran from the eastern flank of Worvas Hill to the cliffs at Porthrepta Beach, was visited by the Rev John Swete in 1780, who found the workings had even then attained a depth of 80 fathoms (480 ft). During the 19th century this became an important mine employing hundreds of workpeople, and in 1869 a man-engine was installed to assist the miners in ascending from the deeper levels. Continuous working was maintained from 1832 until 1877, during which time £533,000 worth of tin and £58,000 worth of copper were produced and £113,000 paid in dividends against £23,000 called up. The mine was reopened in 1906, but closed again after a few years.

East Providence lay on the south-east side of Carbis Valley, one of its shafts closely adjoining Carbis Bay railway station, whilst its adit on the beach is often mistaken for a cave. Smaller and less successful than its celebrated neighbour, this undertaking ceased operations in 1871.

Trelyon Consols, formed by the amalgamation of a number of ancient concerns bearing such names as Trelyon Downs, Wheal Venture and Wheal Widden, lay sandwiched between Wheal Margery on the north and Wheal Providence on the south-east on the eastern flank of Worvas Hill, with an adit draining towards the cliffs north of Porthrepta beach. Between 1849 and 1871 it produced 1,197 tons 8 cwt of tin and 261 tons 18 cwt of copper worth (with sundries) £88,760. The mine was abandoned in 1874.

The sett of Worvas Downs mine occupies the south-west side of Worvas Hill, and at certain periods of its history included also Balnoon. The mine is very old, and in its early days was reputed to be very rich. Around 1810 it was worked by the Daniels of St Ives, and the old burrows proved so valuable that they carried home each day's produce in bags every evening—tin then selling at £35 per ton! The mine was revived for a short time in 1860, and again in 1905, when some expensive equipment was installed. Its epitaph was written in 1912 by Collins, who observed laconically that it had yielded nothing except for the lawyers.

Several mines were formerly to be found in what is now the town of St Ives itself. Wheal Ayr was one of the most interesting of these, and its old engine house, later converted to a private dwelling, formed a picturesque landmark opposite Ayr Terrace until demolished in 1935. When an attempt was made to reopen this mine in 1838 some riotous proceedings took place, the townspeople fearing the loss of their water supply at Venton Ia well, as had happened on a previous occasion.

Some of the old burrows of Wheal Trenwith may still be seen on the southern side of the Stennack valley, behind Rosewall Terrace and Cottages. This began life as a tin and copper mine, and was active in 1812. On May 12, 1826 a cargo of copper ore from Trenwith was loaded into the schooner *Polmanter* at St Ives pier, and on the 16th another into the *Betsey*, the first such shipments made here. In the 1840's some of the Trenwith copper ores were found to be mixed with pitchblende, a mineral then of little value, and the smelters advised the mine that this should be thrown away! Trenwith closed as a copper producer in 1856, but reopened in 1908 as a radium mine, some of its output used by Mme Curie in her experiments. The Great War unfortunately put an end to this interesting venture, as German interests were involved.

Higher up the Stennack lay St Ives Consols, a rich and productive mine. First put to work in a comprehensive way by Sir Christopher Hawkins in 1818 for electioneering purposes, it soon proved to be a most valuable property, and was developed on a large scale by James Halse in the 1820's and '30's. The mine contained some large and unusual ore formations known as 'carbonas,' which, when excavated, produced large caverns, whose roofs had to be supported by massive timbers. In April 1843 a workman's lighted candle stuck against a beam in the fabulously rich 'Great Carbona' caused a disastrous fire which burned for six weeks and led to the destruction of that section of the mine. In 1861 the Rev William Booth—later General Booth of the Salvation Army— who was then conducting a revivalist campaign at St Ives, descended to the 110 fm level and conducted a religious service in another of these carbonas. The mine closed in 1875, but some work was done in the upper levels for a few years after this. Total recorded returns down to 1892 were valued at £1,024,467, whilst tin production (1827-92) amounted to 16,460 tons. Small quantities of copper were also sold. In 1907 the mine was taken over by St Ives Consolidated Mines Ltd, who proposed to work it in conjunction with Trenwith, Rosewall Hill, Giew and Georgia. They built a central power station near the present Leach pottery, but not much work seems to have been done in Consols itself, and the mine closed during the Great War. Giew, however, remained active until 1922, its closing in that year marking the end of the mining industry at St Ives.

Rosewall Hill was the scene of some early mining operations. Ancient 'coffens,' or open cast workings, may still be traced on its summit, following the line of the lodes, and documentary evidence can be found for the existence of a stamping mill and a 'tynnworke' called 'Hard to Come by' here in the 1680's. Ruined engine houses and stacks of the 19th century mine, known as Rosewall Hill and Ransom United, are still prominent features on the eastern side of the hill. Carbonas were also encountered here by the miners; and it is said that a waggon and team of horses might have been turned round in one of them. On the southern side of the hill stands the engine house of another old mine, Wheal Tyringham Consols, whilst the shaft of Wheal Racer is approached by a road at the Buttermilk end of Rosewall. The solitary stack standing in a field near Folly Farm belongs to an old mine known as St Ives Wheal Allen, which was active in the 1860's. The dumps of Goole Pellas adjoin the main road on the north side of Rosewall Hill; this was worked for a time by Rosewall Hill adventurers, but also had a short independent career in the early 1880's using machinery transferred from the defunct Wheal Providence.

Several small mines were opened in the cliffs around St Ives. At Hor Point a few surface remains may still be seen of a romantically situated little enterprise known as Hor Bal or Mungren's Hill mine. Nearer the town, at Man's Head, was Carrack Dhu, whose main period of working lasted from 1853 to 1860, when 1,120 tons of seven per cent copper ore and 5 tons of tin were produced. One of its shafts lies near the old quarry and its adit is to be seen in the cliff just west of Carthew.

At the eastern end of Porthmeor beach was Wheal Snuff, which owed its name to the snuff-coloured 'country' there; and traces of early mining can also be discerned in rocks on the back of the Island. An unsuccessful attempt was made to open a mine at Pednolver Point in 1860, the attractive engine house erected on the edge of the sea being a prominent feature in old photographs of the town taken around 80 years ago.

Lelant possessed a large number of mines, ranging in size from the extensive Wheal Sisters (incorporating Wheals Margaret, Mary and Kitty) to little 'bals' like West Lucy, above Hayle river, and Fanny Adela, at Hawke's Point. The scarred countryside between Trencrom and Nancledra bears mute witness to the great importance of this industry in the last century, and many people can still remember the noisy stamps, powered by waterwheels, at work in the valleys crushing stuff retrieved from the old mine burrows in the 1920's and 30's. In Trevarrack valley these were located at Treva, Mennor, Trevarrack, Bowl Rock and Trink, and in Nancledra valley at Lock.

Wheal Reeth, on Trink Hill, was an exceptionally interesting old mine. A primitive 'fire engine' was installed here as early as 1748 whose top speed was only seven strokes per minute, yet when working only half her time sufficed to draw all the water. Abandoned around 1772 through dissensions among the adventurers, the mine was reopened by James Halse in 1822, and proved so profitable that it laid the foundations of his great fortune. Davies Gilbert, the Cornish historian, stated in 1838 that Wheal Reeth had been more productive of tin than any other mine hitherto except Wheal Vor.

Zennor could boast of no large mines, the reason apparently being that although the lodes in that parish were often exceptionally rich they also tended to be rather small. Probably the best known of them was the old Morvah and Zennor United, whose mournfully evocative ruins set against a dramatic backdrop of rugged hills, cliffs and the sea at Carn Galver form a notable feature alongside the St Ives to Land's End coastal road.

ABOVE: Carbis Valley, c1880 with the ruined engine house of East Providence on the right (HF; EA); BELOW: Wheal Trenwith, c1850. (RIC)

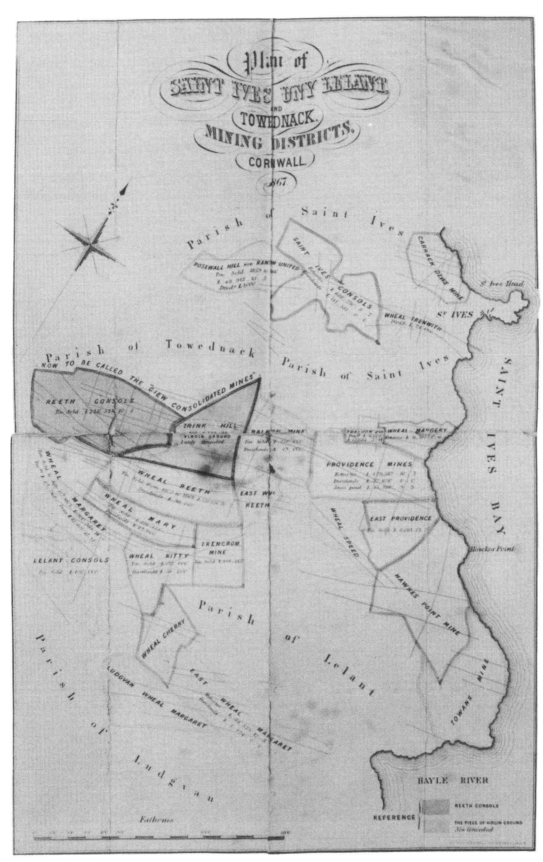

The mining district of St Ives, uny Lelant and Towednack in 1867.
(CRO; WT)

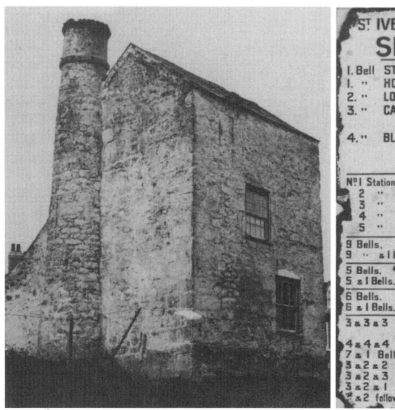

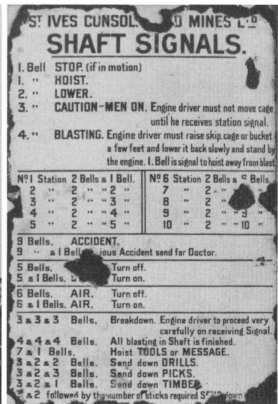

ST. IVES CUNSOL___ ___ ___D MINES L.D
SHAFT SIGNALS.

1. Bell	STOP. (if in motion)
1. "	HOIST.
2. "	LOWER.
3. "	CAUTION—MEN ON. Engine driver must not move cage until he receives station signal.
4. "	BLASTING. Engine driver must raise skip, cage or bucket a few feet and lower it back slowly and stand by the engine. I. Bell is signal to hoist away from blast.

N⁰ 1 Station 2 Bells & 1 Bell.			N⁰ 6 Station 2 Bells & 6 Bells.		
2 "	2 "	2	7 "	2 "	
3 "	2 "	3	8 "	2 "	
4 "	2 "	4	9 "	2 "	9
5 "	2 "	5	10 "	2 "	10

| 9 Bells. | ACCIDENT. |
| 9 " & 1 Bell ___ ious Accident send for Doctor. | |

| 5 Bells. | Turn off. |
| 5 & 1 Bells. | Turn on. |

| 6 Bells. AIR. | Turn off. |
| 6 & 1 Bells. AIR. | Turn on. |

3 & 3 & 3 Bells.	Breakdown. Engine driver to proceed very carefully on receiving Signal.
4 & 4 & 4 Bells.	All blasting in Shaft is finished.
7 & 1 Bells.	Hoist TOOLS or MESSAGE.
3 & 2 & 2 Bells.	Send down DRILLS.
3 & 2 & 3 Bells.	Send down PICKS.
3 & 2 & 1 Bells.	Send down TIMBER.
___ & 2 followed by the number of sticks required S___ down	

LEFT: Ayr engine house; RIGHT: 1910 shaft signals at St Ives Consolidated Mines (M; WT); and BELOW: the miners of Trenwith November 28, 1912. (M; HJH)

ABOVE: Children and bal maidens working at St Ives Consols, c1870
(RIC); BELOW: blacksmith's shop at Consols. (RIC)

ABOVE: Zennor Mill; BELOW: Hawke's Point 1880 with Edward and Elizabeth Ashton's cottage where he lived over 50 years mining nickel and cobalt; years previously, William Bottrell lived a lone life with his cat Spriggans, pony and cow (HF; EA); INSET: Bowl Rock Stamps, Lelant, in the 1920's. (M)

Fair Play

The progress of the seasons at St Ives was formerly marked by a succession of quaint customs and ceremonies, many of which still survive. In early spring comes 'Feast,' held on the nearest Sunday to February 3, the anniversary of the dedication of the Parish Church. Lelant Feast falls on February 2, so that the two events usually coincide. This made it possible for St Ives to play Lelant at hurling on their common holiday of Feast Monday. Indeed, in early times the parish of Ludgvan also joined in, by virtue of the fact that it then formed part of the living of St Ives.

The silver hurling ball used to be thrown to the players near a stone marking the St Ives and Lelant parish boundary at Chyangweal, the two 'goals' being their respective parish churches. The winning side kept possession of the ball until the following year. As the population of St Ives increased, Lelant began to find itself outnumbered in the game, and dropped out. Hurling was thereafter confined to the young men of St Ives, who played it on the Fore Sand between Pednolver and Castle Rock, dividing themselves into two teams, as follows:

> Toms, Wills and Jans
> Take off all's on the san's—

that is, all named Thomas, John or William were ranged on one side, those of any other Christian name on the other. A pole was erected on the beach, and each side strove to reach the 'goold' oftenest, their opponents struggling to keep them out and as far from it as possible.

The game thus continued to be played for many years; but then a decline set in, the pole disappeared, and it became merely a romp for children, the Mayor presenting a reward of five shillings to the boy or girl who returned the ball promptly at noon. In 1972, however, the Mayor (Keith Slocombe) reorganised the event, reviving its old spirit and character. Early on Feast Monday the silver ball was carried in state to the holy well of St Ia at Porthmeor, where it was immersed and blessed. The ball was borne on a cushion of ivy through the old part of the town in a procession headed by a boy drummer, which included the Vicar, Town Crier and mace bearers. Following a reception at the Guildhall, the Mayor headed a larger procession to the churchyard, where he stood on the wall and threw the ball to the waiting players below with the cry in Cornish 'Guare wheg ya guare teg' (fair play is good play.) The teams represented the two ancient divisions and rivalries of St Ives— 'Uplong' and 'Downlong,' the former wearing red favours and the latter white. The Downlong goal (a basket ball net on a post) was at Smeaton's Pier end of the harbour beach, and the Uplong goal on Porthminster Beach. The tide being in, and little sand available, the game was played mainly in the streets of the town. After the ball had been returned to the Guildhall, the Mayor threw handfuls of twopenny pieces from the balcony to the children in the forecourt.

The ball consists of a round piece of wood or cork, about the size of an orange, covered with a thin layer of silver. This metal used to be obtained from silver coins collected from door to door by boys some days beforehand and put around the ball by a local silversmith. During recent years the Feast celebrations have been diversified by a meet of the Western Hunt in the morning and a football match during the afternoon.

Soon after Feast comes Shrove Tuesday. Dr Robert Hunt has recorded how the boys of St Ives would tie stones to cords and with these parade the town, striking them against doors and shouting

'Give me a pancake, now—now—now,
Or I'll souse in your door with a row—tow—tow.'

This is one custom whose passing need hardly be regretted.

Visitors to St Ives have often remarked on the seeming anomaly of Good Friday being observed in this strongly religious, indeed Puritan town by the sailing of model boats on pools not merely by children but their elders also. The origins of the custom are, in fact, religious, the object being to give symbolic protection to the family's fishing boat during the coming year. The late R. Morton Nance stated that the only other place where it has been observed in recent times is Sark, in the Channel Islands, but it was probably once a common practice. Possibly the traditional eating of fish on Fridays which was so helpful to their calling, made fishermen specially fix on Good Friday for this ceremony; or it may coincide with the time of year, at the beginning of their summer season, when, in pagan times, they sent miniature boats to sea, hoping that this offering would be accepted and their own boats spared.

Formerly this model boat sailing took place on the Cock Bank Pool, a long stretch of water which, at low tide, used to extend from Smeaton's Pier to Pednolver Point, inside the large sand bank known as the 'Ridge'. The models included luggers, brigs and schooners, as well as yachts; and they were not carved from blocks of wood, as today, but built with planks, just like the real thing. In later years the venue was transferred to the mine engine ponds at Wheal Speed and Consols, and is now confined to the latter.

Towednack Feast occurs on the Sunday nearest to April 28, and is sometimes called the 'crowder' feast, because the fiddler led a procession from the church door through the village to a tune on his 'crowd'. It is also known as 'Cuckoo Feast,' as it is then that the cuckoo is usually first heard in the district. It was unkindly said at St Ives that Towednack people built a hedge around the cuckoo to stop it flying away, so they might have summer always with them; to this, the Towednackians responded with the allegation that St Ives fishermen had whipped a hake through the town to teach its fellows not to steal pilchards from their nets. St Ives people are called 'Hakes' to this day—an appellation they do not greatly appreciate.

May Day was celebrated by the blowing of tin trumpets, known as May horns, together with whistles and 'pee-weeps' made from young branches of sycamore or May trees by cutting a circle through the bark, which was beaten to loosen it and slipped off the wood. An angular cut was made at the end of the wood to form a mouthpiece, and both the wood and bark slit, making a whistle when reunited. The May horns are now silent; but Midsummer Eve is still marked by lighting a bonfire on one of the adjacent hills—part of a chain which blazes across Cornwall from Land's End to the Tamar as dusk descends. This is an ancient ceremony connected with Sun worship, though now superficially Christianised.

The Knill ceremony takes place only once every five years on St James' day (July 25). Ten little girls dressed in white, accompanied by two elderly widows, and led by a fiddler, go in procession from the Guildhall to the Malakoff, from where they are taken by coach to Trelyon, completing the journey to the top of Worvas Hill on foot. Here, watched by thousands of spectators, the children trip around a fifty foot high granite pyramid or mausoleum to the tune of the Cornish Furry Dance, and at the end of a quarter of an hour stand and sing the metrical version of the Old Hundredth Psalm—'All people that on earth do dwell.' With them appear the Mayor, Vicar and Customs Officer—the trustees—and a Master of Ceremonies.

This quaint ceremony was originated by John Knill, Collector of Customs at St Ives from 1762-82, and Mayor in 1767. Though not a native—he was born at Callington in 1733—he developed a great affection for St Ives and its people, for whom he was able to perform several valuable services, including the erection of Smeaton's Pier. In his will he expressed a desire to be remembered a little longer than in usual with those of whom there is no ostensible memorial. Accordingly, in 1782, he built his celebrated steeple; and in 1797 drew up a trust deed containing the necessary provisions for the quinquennial ceremony.

This first took place in 1801, and Mr Knill was actually present himself on the occasion. To meet all the charges involved, including the upkeep of the mausoleum, Knill settled an annuity of £10 on the trustees, as a rent charge paid by the manor of Gluvian, in Mawgan. The money was deposited in an iron chest, secured by three locks, to which each trustee had a key. At the end of each five-year period, £25 of the accumulated money was to be laid out on the ceremony. The trustees had £10 for a dinner, the girls received £5 between them, the fiddler £1 and the widows £1 each. Provision was also made for a number of other charitable bequests, but these have lapsed in consequence of the greatly altered value of money.

The children taking part must be natives of the borough and daughters of seamen, fishermen or tinners, none of them exceeding ten years of age. Money was provided for breast knots for them and the widows and a cockade for the fiddler. The monument is a triangular pyramid set on a square base. It bears Knill's coat of arms, with the motto *Resurgam*, and the text 'I know that my Redeemer liveth.' The structure is hollow; and on the south side is a low arch which is periodically opened to give a view of the interior. The cavity contains a stone sarcophagus in which Knill intended to be interred, but difficulties regarding consecration made this impossible, and following his death in 1811 at his chambers in Gray's Inn Square, he was buried in London.

Knill led an interesting and varied life. In 1773 he made an inspection of the Jamaican ports for Government, and in 1777 was appointed private secretary to the Duke of Buckinghamshire, taking rooms in Dublin Castle when that nobleman became Lord Lieutenant of Ireland. He also speculated in a search for treasure supposed to have been hidden near the Lizard by the notorious pirate Avery. He is said to have equipped some small vessels to act as privateers against smugglers, but according to local tradition was himself a 'Free Trader.' As an occasional visitor to the 'George and Dragon' inn in the Market Place, he concocted, together with his punch, many a little scheme for landing contraband cargoes.

Knill was, in fact, believed to be in league with pirates, wreckers and smugglers, and to have erected his mausoleum as a daymark for their craft. Around the middle of the 18th century a vessel was wrecked on the eastern side of Carrack Gladden, and the crew, after getting ashore, quickly disappeared. The ship was full of china and other smuggled goods, whilst her papers were removed and burnt, supposedly because they implicated Knill and Squire Praed of Trevetho. The customs officer, Roger Wearne, went on board and stuffed his clothes full of china. Several beautiful pieces were concealed in the seat of his breeches, and as he was getting down the ship's side, someone gave him a sound blow with a stick from behind, smashing them to atoms. These, however, may be but idle tales. They certainly do not accord with what is factually known about Knill's career. He was, in short, a distinguished public servant, a highly regarded member of the legal profession, and an adviser to the Government in several different capacities.

Very different in character from the picturesque formalism and charm of the Knill ceremony is the 'Crying the Neck' which takes place at harvest time. The 'neck' consists of the last few stalks of standing corn, which are cut by a scythe and held aloft, the reaper crying 'What have I?' three times, to which the onlookers reply 'A neck! A neck! A neck!' In olden days this would be followed by a 'gooldize' or harvest supper.

On Allhallows Eve many children are still given a large apple, which they place under their pillows when going to bed, and eat the following morning. This day is known at St Ives as 'Allan Apple Day,' and so great was the demand for these apples that they were sold at a special 'Allan Market.'

By its ancient Charter St Ives was granted four annual fairs; the only one which survived into this century was that authorised for December 3 and 4. In practice, it was always held on a Saturday and the Monday following, and called 'Fair Mo', meaning 'Pig Fair'. Pigs were kept in large numbers in the 'Pigs' Towns' at the Breakwater and Porthmeor, their meat being sold at 'standings' in the streets. It was largely patronised by the fishermen and miners, but in later years became largely an occasion for the children, being given over

ABOVE LEFT: Hurling to g
old days (PQ); CENTRE: da
ball (BELOW) at Venton
hurling 1975-style (WT); BE
the 1890's, J. H. Tremayne
carol *Uncle John* composed an
80 St Ives carol choir (TM

to the sale of 'clidgey,' fruit, gingerbread, coconuts and toys. The fair lingered on until 1938, when two stalls were erected outside the Library; but black-out restrictions the following year led to its suspension, and it has never been revived.

Christmas has always been kept up with great spirit at St Ives. Local carols, such as the famous 'Hellesveor,' composed by blind ex-miner Colan ('Cully') Williams are still sung in the chapels and streets with much enthusiasm. On Christmas Day itself large numbers of children used to assemble at Porthminster Beach and play rounders, kiss-in-the-ring and 'Thurza.' At Zennor, the young women would rise early to wash the family's clothes and get them dry against Christmas, the hedges near their homes being covered with snow-white linen, much to their credit—hence the saying 'If you want a good wife, go to Zennor for her.'

'Guise Dancing' was celebrated during the twelve days of Christmas. Young people would dress up in all manner of fancy costumes, and, with their faces covered, visit their friends—and sometimes their enemies—in companies, and dance, and exchange pleasantries in high falsetto voices, hoping to escape recognition. They were usually entertained with a drink and some seasonal fare before proceeding to the next house, where the performance was repeated. The streets wore a carnival aspect, and tradesmen shuttered their shops early on account of the uproar, noise and general misbehaviour. The custom died out between the Wars, but has recently been revived as part of the Feast Monday celebrations.

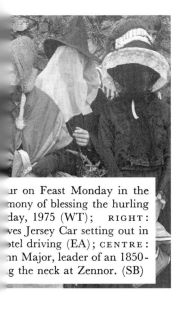

...ur on Feast Monday in the ...mony of blessing the hurling ...day, 1975 (WT); RIGHT: ...ves Jersey Car setting out in ...tel driving (EA); CENTRE: ...n Major, leader of an 1850- ...g the neck at Zennor. (SB)

SHEPHERDS

Music by J. MAJOR, St Ives
TUNE UNCLE JOHN

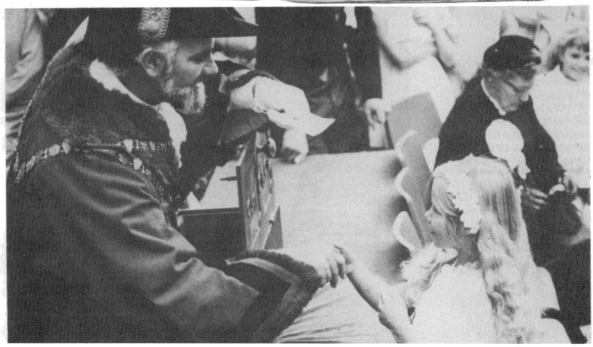

ABOVE: Knill Trustees' account book 1801—the first ceremony (TC);
BELOW: Margaret Sedgeman receives her Knill bequest in 1971 from
Mayor T. K. Slocombe. (WT)

106

LEFT: The 1881 celebration, John Major, fiddler; RIGHT: John Care, fiddler, leads the girls around the steeple in the 1976 ceremony. (WT)
BELOW: the Hellesveor Choir of 1911. (M)

Back row (left to right): T. Welch (cornet), Miss J. Nicholls (Mrs White), Miss Murt (Mrs T. Leddra), J. Tanner, S. Cocking, T. Curnow, D. Uren (clarionette), D. Martin, Miss M. T. Couch (Mrs Stevens), Miss T. Rowe (Mrs Nicholls), C. Major (violin). Second row: W. Stevens (collector), Miss S. Woolcock, Miss J. Matthews (Mrs. W. Berriman), Miss A. Martin (Mrs Martin), W. H. Care, Miss A. Williams (Mrs Hocking), Colan ('Cully') Williams (leader), Miss M. Thomas (Mrs Cowling), W. Matthews, Miss Curnow, P. Berriman, Miss L. Noall (Mrs S. Berriman), Miss M. A. Batten (Mrs W. Stevens), Miss E. Barber (Mrs Vincent). Third row: R. Tanner, Miss E. C. Williams, Miss P. Chard (Mrs Thomas), Miss F. Kemp (Mrs Murt), C. Williams (junior), Miss E. Noall (Mrs Richards), Miss R. Berriman (Mrs Wills), Miss A. Phillips (Mrs H. Fleming), Miss L. Berriman (Mrs A. Trewhella), Miss E. Polmeor (Mrs W. Trevorrow), Miss A. Berriman (Mrs N. Carbines), Miss C. Curnow (Mrs G. Phillips), Mr Buzza. Front row: S. Noall, H. Curnow, H. Burrell, C. Beckerleg, C. Pearce, J. Thomas, E. Curnow, C. Nicholls, R. J. Noall.

EDUCA

Wm. THOMAS

Hereby notices his intention to open a

SCHOOL

AT

HALSETOWN,

On Monday the 4th day of May, 1840,

For the purpose of Instruction, at the following Charges:

	PER QUARTER.
	s. d.
Reading and Spelling - - -	2 6
Writing - - - - -	5 0
Arithmetic - - - - -	7 6

And as soon as a youth gets advanced to either of the following studies, the extra charge will be

FOR	PER QUARTER,
Grammar - - - - -	2 6
Geography - - - -	2 6
Use of Globes - - - -	2 6
Navigatio - - - -	5 0
Mensura on - - - -	2 6
Geomet - - - -	2 6
Algebra - - - - -	2 6
Euclid's Elements - -	2 6

W. T. having been 2 or 3 Years with Mr. PHILLIPS, (late Teacher in this neighbourhood) avails himself of the same process of Instruction; having also assisted him largely in Land-surveying, he undertak to instruct young me in the Rudiments of these department reasonable Terms.

An EVENING will be commenced at the usua. ason of the year.

Instead of he cus ary Midsu mer holida s, it is proposed to give 3 We in August, on account of the Harvest season.

Dated, 24th Apr , 18 0.

R. K. , Printer, Bookbind & Stationer, St. Ives.

A private school opens at Halsetown in 1840. (M)

Now and Then

Although a railway to St Ives had been projected as early as 1844, it was not until May 1874 that a contract for building the line was signed. Its promoters were the Associated Companies. It took almost exactly three years to complete. The $4\frac{1}{2}$ mile long branch from St Ives Road (now St Erth) station on the West Cornwall Railway was ceremonially opened with the arrival at St Ives of a decorated train drawn by the engine *Elephant* on May 24, 1877. A regular service for goods began on May 28 and for passengers on June 1. The line is historically interesting in being the last ever built to Brunel's famous broad gauge of 7 ft $0\frac{1}{4}$ ins, converted to standard gauge in 1892. It is a most beautiful route, running first by the side of the Hayle estuary, then across Lelant Towans and through the deep Carrack Gladden cutting to Carbis Bay, crossing the valley by a graceful viaduct, and so winding around the cliffs to St Ives with superb coastal views all the way.

The line greatly assisted the fishing industry by expediting the despatch of fish, but brought about the decline of the port, filching trade from the little coasting schooners and ketches. It made possible the development of the tourist industry, and so initiated that process of change leading to the building of hotels and boarding houses and the conversion of many ancient buildings to satisfy the requirements, real or imagined, of the holiday-maker.

First to appreciate the potential of the new tourist industry was the Great Western Railway, which in 1877 acquired Tregenna Castle and opened it as an hotel. The publicity they lavished on this hotel and on St Ives played a significant part in popularising the resort. Many improvements were required to bring the town's amenities up to the standard of a high class watering place. Fortunately, in the period before the first World War local affairs were largely directed by men of vision who realised what needed to be done, and carried it out effectively. During the 1880's and 1890's an extensive drainage system was installed and the inadequate water supplies derived from Wheal Ayr and the Fountain or Trenwith adit were supplemented by a reservoir on Hellesveor Moors fed by the stream flowing from Wheal Allen and in summer by pumping from the deep levels of Consols mine. In 1908, when Wheal Trenwith and St Ives Consols were taken over by a new mining company, depriving the town of supplies from those sources, the Corporation was obliged to construct a new reservoir at Bussow, which was opened on March 28, 1910. With the closing of the mines during the War, the Trenwith supply again became available, and in 1932 this was linked to a new covered reservoir at Worvas Hill for supplying Carbis Bay. Since then, this reservoir has received an alternative supply from old mines at Amalveor Downs.

The wonderful golden beaches of St Ives, so deservedly popular with present-day visitors, presented a different aspect a century ago—sadly neglected and used only by fishermen. Porthminster, most beautiful of them all, had been disfigured by hundreds of tons of stone dumped on it by the railway contractors, whilst on the green above scores of large, broad-beamed, tar-coated seine boats were drawn up, their sides torn, ribs rotting and exposed timbers bleaching in the rain and sun. However, by the 1880's ladies' bathing tents had been installed on the beach, whilst the men and boys had staked out exclusive bathing rights to Pednolver rocks, mixed bathing being unheard-of in those days! The beach was purchased by the Corporation in 1920, but it was not until 1928 that the last seine boats disappeared, the putting green, sea wall and other features appearing in the early 1930's.

Porthmeor was marred by its gasworks and notorious Pigs' Town, whose combined odours not even the Atlantic breezes could dispel. Of late years this beach has become increasingly popular, especially with surfers, whilst Porthgwidden has been transformed from a small fishing cove into an attractive bathing beach, though some of the old natural charm has gone. Even the once dirty harbour, littered with coal from trading vessels, has now been partly taken over by the bucket and spade fraternity, whilst the rocky beach below the church also has its devotees.

The Island, which owed its preservation from development to the practice of fishermen spreading their nets on its emerald turf to dry, was purchased by the Council in 1906 for £650. They were likewise fortunate in obtaining the picturesque headland of Carrack Dhu (Carthew) as a gift from T. Bedford Bolitho, of Trengwainton, in 1902. An Act of Parliament secured the coast from Carthew to Clodgy for the town in 1930, when the necessary land was acquired by compulsory purchase from various owners.

In 1896 Mr Bolitho gave the Corporation a piece of land below the Coastguard Station on Porthminster Point, which was then laid out with footpaths and shrubs to form a semi-wild pleasure ground, to a design by F. W. Meyer, the landscape gardener, of Exeter. Much more recently, the National Trust was given the cliffs below the railway between Porthminster Point and Carbis Bay, and also has a covenant over Hellesveor Cliffs. In 1933 Mrs Elizabeth ('Granny') Ashton announced her intention of presenting to the town a beautiful section of coastline at Hawke's Point, which included the Nut Grove, St Uny's well and the Grotto. This last feature was unfortunately destroyed in the last War to make way for a gun emplacement. In this manner a substantial amount of the glorious coastal scenery around St Ives has been preserved for posterity, but there have been serious losses—in particular, at the Hain Walk and in parts of Carbis Bay.

On the cultural side, an important development was the opening of a public library at the Passmore Edwards Institute in Gabriel Street on April 20, 1897. The foundation stone had been laid a year before (April 29, 1896) by the donor, J. Passmore Edwards, a wealthy Cornish-born newspaper proprietor, on a site given by T. B. Bolitho, MP, the architects Messrs Symons and Son, of Blackwater. For many years the Council used the upper floor for their meetings, but in 1951 the St Ives Museum was opened here. Following the transference of the Museum to the former Seamen's Mission at Wheal Dream in 1968, the Passmore Edwards Institute was completely remodelled internally by H. C. Gilbert, and the library (now a branch of Cornwall County Library) improved to a high standard by J. K. Mealor, the last Borough Librarian.

In 1927 Mrs Elizabeth Noy, of St Ives, bequeathed 5,000 guineas for the erection of a new municipal building. This resulted in the opening in 1940 of the Guildhall in Street-an-Pol, an attractive edifice with a balcony overlooking a spacious forecourt, which has served the town well, the concert hall being a particularly valuable amenity. Its erection unfortunately entailed the demolition of a gracious old Georgian house, known as The Retreat, which possessed, among other features, an Adams fireplace. The architect was Capt G. B. Drewitt, and the builders Messrs John Williams & Co (Cornwall) Ltd. Its total cost, including equipment, amounted to £20,502.

One of the most popular local institutions before the second World War was the Volunteer Fire Brigade. The sight of the firemen wearing their brass helmets—the captain's was silver—hastening on their engine to an outbreak excited general admiration, and of course no carnival or procession was complete without them. There is a record of money subscribed in 1854 for the purchase of a fire engine, and in 1867 Mr William Roberts enquired of the Mayor of Penzance particulars regarding the remuneration given to members of the Penzance brigade, as the St Ives Lighting Inspectors were contemplating the establishment of a brigade here. However, the fire-fighting arrangements devised for the town were far from satisfactory, as was painfully evident in 1889 when a conflagration in the Digey claimed the lives of three little girls. As a result, a volunteer fire brigade was formed in May 1890. Their uniform consisted of a blue serge tunic and trousers, brass helmet, belt and axe, and they made their first public appearance at the opening ceremony of the Smeaton's Pier extension in June. The old manual fire engine and dilapidated equipment handed over to them were almost past service; in 1893 a practically new 22-manual fire engine was purchased from Messrs Shand, Mason & Co for £100, and christened 'St Ia' by Miss Gracie Hain, daughter of Sir E. Hain, in August of that year. During the 1939-45 War this machine, then obsolete after its replacement by a motor fire engine in 1928, was taken to Consols to be used as a road block in the event of an invasion. It was later broken up, and the writer saw two of its wheels lying in a field at Halsetown some years ago. An interesting event occurred in July 1908, when Capt John Pearce, of the St Ives Brigade, welcomed the firemen of Cornwall to a reception at Treloyhan Manor, their hosts being Mr and Mrs Hain. Over 200 officers and men were present, all in full dress, presenting a quite remarkable spectacle. A similar gathering took place in July 1930, when nearly 300 officers and men from 21 Cornish brigades with several fire engines, and headed by St Ives Silver Band, paraded from the railway station to the War Memorial and then to the Island, where they were received by the Mayor, Coun.W. Craze. The St Ives brigade gave yeoman service, attending a number of serious fires, during one of which, at Virgin Street, in April 1921, Fireman W. P. Uren lost his life.

The St Ives District Nursing Association was formed in October 1892 to engage a trained nurse who attended patients in their homes, the work being carried on with the aid of donations and subscriptions. The St John Ambulance Brigade was established in May 1902, although first aid examinations had been held some years before. The first motor ambulance was bought in March 1922, and a motor ambulance service provided until 1976, when the County ambulances took over. After Sir Edward Hain's son, Capt Edward Hain, was killed at Gallipoli in the Great War, the shareholders of the Hain Steamship Co voted £5,000 to provide a memorial to him, which took the form of the Edward Hain Memorial Cottage Hospital. In 1919 Albany House, formerly the residence of Mrs Morris, was purchased, and with the help of an endowment of £8,000 provided by Lady Hain, the hospital was opened by her on April 8, 1920.

St Ives is world famous as an art centre. The first artists of any importance who worked in the town were Whistler and his friend Walter Sickert, who passed the winter of 1884 here; the Newlyn art colony had been founded a few years earlier. Old sail lofts and cottages were converted into studios, whilst large skylights appeared everywhere among the grey roofs of the old town. From its earliest days the colony has had a truly cosmopolitan character, artists from all over the world settling here and exhibiting their works in many countries. Among the pioneers were W. H. Y. Titcomb, Julius Olsson, Arnesby Brown, Adrian Stokes, E. W. Blomefield, William Eadie and H. H. Robinson.

In 1887 a small picture gallery was opened by J. K. Lanham above his shop in High Street where he sold artists' materials. The St Ives Society of Artists, formed in 1927, opened their Porthmeor Gallery in 1928. This proved successful, and in 1947 the Society moved to the former Mariners' Church in Norway Lane, which they purchased from the Church Council a few years later. Its membership has included Moffat Lindner, Capt Borlase Smart, Sir Alfred Munnings, S. J. Lamorna Birch, Claude Muncaster and Hugh Ridge.

Tensions between 'traditionalists' and 'modernists' in the Society led to the latter breaking away in 1949 and setting up the Penwith Society of Arts. They now have an excellent gallery in Back Roads converted from an old fish cellar. Membership is not restricted to painters, sculptors and other craftsmen also being eligible. Among those who joined the Society were Sven Berlin, Leonard Fuller, Barbara Hepworth, Peter Lanyon, Bernard Leach, Dicon and Robin Nance, Ben Nicholson, Herbert Read, Shearer Armstrong, and Misome Peile.

The St Ives Arts Club pre-dates both these societies. Founded in 1890, it occupies a quaint half-timbered building set on the seawall at Westcott's Quay, where it is often drenched by spray in rough weather. The ground floor was formerly a seine cellar owned by the eccentric Mr Eathorne, who would sometimes put out an anchor to prevent its being washed away! The club forms a social centre for painters and others, and is noted for its dramatic productions.

In 1938 Leonard Fuller established the St Ives School of Painting, whose influence has been far-reaching. Following his death in 1973 the school was carried on by his wife, Marjorie Mostyn.

Prior to the Second World War annual 'Show Days' were held, when artists opened their studios to the public and displayed works intended for the Royal Academy.

Special mention must be made of our trio of 'local' painters—Alfred Wallis, Peter Lanyon and Bryan Pearce. Wallis, a self-taught 'primitive,' began painting at the age of seventy, using house paints and pieces of cardboard cut from packing cases. He delighted in views of St Ives harbour, depicting the quay, lighthouses and fishing boats with a child-like clarity of vision. He died at Madron Workhouse in 1942, and is commemorated by a slate tablet on the small cottage at 3, Back Road West where he lived and painted many of his pictures, whilst his grave at Barnoon cemetery is marked by an unusual tiled stone designed by Bernard Leach featuring a lighthouse.

Peter Lanyon was greatly influenced by the wild, rugged scenery of the Penwith peninsula, which he transformed on his canvases into bold, compelling abstractions. His career was cut tragically short by a gliding accident in 1964.

Bryan Pearce provides an inspiring example of a severe personal handicap courageously overcome, and in his paintings of St Ives he has achieved a distinct, indeed unique style, his work being widely praised by discriminating judges.

Two other members of the colony have brought particular renown to St Ives. Bernard Leach studied pottery making in Japan, and then, with the Japanese potter Hamada set up a co-operative pottery at the higher Stennack in 1920. His beautiful domestic stoneware and porcelain soon won international acclaim, and many thousands of visitors have called at the Leach pottery to study the techniques used. Dame Barbara Hepworth likewise gained a worldwide reputation with her abstract sculptured 'shapes and forms.' Following her tragic death in a fire in May 1975 her Trewyn studio home and garden were opened as a museum in 1976, with many examples of her work on display.

Only a brief review of the principal events of the last 100 years can be given here. One of the pleasantest celebrations held during this time was that of Queen Victoria's Golden Jubilee in June 1887. Fishing boats in the harbour displayed bunting and the town was decorated with flags. In the afternoon Capt T. R. Harry entertained over 200 people in the Public Hall, whilst in the evening there was a 'monster' bonfire near Knill's Steeple, followed by a torchlight procession into the town. Free teas were provided for the schoolchildren and old people, whilst a firework display took place on the Malakoff. At Lelant, children from the National and Board Schools attended a service at the Church, after which they marched in procession through the decorated village to Trevetho Park, headed by Hayle Fife and Drum Band and Lelant Downs Brass Band. Tea was provided for nearly a thousand, followed by sports and a donkey race, whilst at dusk fire balloons were sent up. A bonfire lit on Trencrom Hill got out of control, and threatened to destroy the Trevetho plantation.

In 1892 Mr (later Sir) Edward Hain's new residence at Treloyhan was completed by Messrs Lang & Sons to the design of Silvanus Trevail of Truro. It was built of stone quarried at Castle-an-Dinas, about three miles from Penzance, the main doorway on the western side being finely carved. Following Lady Hain's death in 1927, the house was sold, re-opening as a hotel in 1930. During the Second World War pupils of the Downs School, evacuated to St Ives from Seaford, Sussex, were accommodated here. In 1947 the building was acquired by the Wesley Guild as a guest house, and officially opened on March 31, 1948.

During the early 1890's St Ives experienced a number of incidents resulting from vagaries of the weather—the 1891 blizzard, the 'Cintra' gale of November 1893 when three steamers were wrecked at Carbis Bay and one at St Ives, and the great flood of November 12, 1894. Several days' heavy rain culminated in a cloudburst, and water poured in torrents from the surrounding hills into the town, flooding houses and shops and causing much damage to roads. Boats were rowed through the streets rescuing people from their homes, but fortunately no loss of life occurred.

Victoria's Diamond Jubilee in 1897 was marked by a procession of 1,400 children to Higher Tregenna, where an open-air tea was provided, and by a huge bonfire of old seine boats lit in the evening at Trenwith. A more permanent commemoration took the form of a Mayoral chain and badge of 18 ct gold bought by public subscription. The badge is vesica-shaped, with scroll ornaments on the border. In the centre appears the foliated shield of the borough—an ivy branch—with the colours reversed, the leaves being in silver upon a green field. Round the border appears the usual Latin legend while beyond this is a shoal of pilchards. On the reverse is engraved 'Edward Hain, Mayor 1884, 1885, 1886, 1889, 1895, 1899.'

The centre link is made to harmonise with the badge, with a shield 'W. T. 1894', while on the reverse is engraved 'Matthew Trewhella, Mayor, 1847.' On either side of the centre link are two maces in the style of the ancient ones of the borough. These are followed by the 25 sets of links. The chain was worn by the Mayor, Capt T. R. Harry, at a reception for provincial Mayors given by Queen Victoria at Buckingham Palace during the Jubilee celebrations.

During the Great War the men of St Ives achieved a magnificent record of service; and with the return of peace a War Memorial was erected on a central site facing the parish church. Some years before (1908) Sir Edward Hain had laid out the area as a pleasure ground, and the War Memorial was erected in the northern part of this garden. It took the form of a Celtic cross in Cornish granite with a scroll design. The main inscription reads: 'In Proud and Grateful Memory of the Men of St Ives who in the Great War, 1914-1918, gave their all, and in giving raised Men's Ideals of what Man may become. Their name liveth for evermore.' Bronze plaques at the sides carry the names of the fallen; and on the south side is the inscription 'Lest we forget.' The unveiling ceremony was performed on November 2, 1922 by Lady Hain. In 1930 Mrs Bullivant (Sir Edward Hain's daughter) gave the Memorial Gardens to the Corporation. On Remembrance Sunday, 1946, an addition to the memorial recording the names of those who died in the Second World War was unveiled by the Mayor, Coun C. E. Pearce.

A valuable amenity provided by public subscription was opened in 1925—the Recreation Ground at Alexandra Road. This involved the acquisition of 6½ acres of land, which were laid out for cricket, football, hockey and tennis at a cost of nearly £1,000. A similar sum was required for making the new approach road, some of the land needed being given by W. Craze. Local ex-Servicemen provided the wooden grandstand (destroyed by fire during the 'drought' summer of 1976) whilst Mrs Wheeler gave the pavilion in memory of her husband. Alderman S. C. Beckerleg, Chairman of the Recreation Ground Committee, handed over the ground to the Mayor, Alderman M. W. Couch, on April 2, 1925. The St Ives Rugby Football Club have since been given exclusive use of this ground, and in March 1968 opened a large clubhouse there. The iron entrance gates were erected in memory of Harry Oliver, one of St Ives' most brilliant footballers.

The inter-war years brought many changes—the construction of large Council housing estates at Bullan's Lane and Ayr; the demolition, despite many protests, of such well-loved features as Pudding Bag Lane and The Retreat; the arrival, in the early '20's, of the Great Western and CMT 'buses, whose vigorous competition caused both amusement and irritation to passengers; the building of Wharf Road in 1922; and then, in the late 1930's, the comprehensive new drainage scheme, including Carbis Bay, which made necessary the construction of Pednolver Walk and large holding tanks at the Wharf.

In 1934 the Borough of St Ives was enlarged by including the districts of Lelant and Carbis Bay. To mark this event, a second medallion was added to the Mayor's chain. It consists of a representation of the Borough Seal (1690) with, on the reverse, the inscription: 'Greater St Ives, 1934. Lelant, Carbis Bay and District.'

St Ives suffered two air raids in the Second World War. The first occurred during the night of January 25, 1941, when a German plane dropped two bombs in the upper part of the Stennack, one—a parachute landmine—falling near the Leach pottery and the other in a field not far from St John's Vicarage. One house was demolished, and others, including the church and vicarage, badly damaged, whilst several people were slightly injured. This plane also machine-gunned the town. The second attack took place in daylight on the afternoon of August 28, 1942 when a plane scored a direct hit on Porthmeor gasworks, putting it out of action for several weeks, and dropped a second bomb at the top of Porthmeor Hill. A number of people on Porthmeor Beach were injured by bomb fragments and debris, whilst a woman was killed outside her bungalow, her daughter also sustaining severe injuries. Property at Godrevy Terrace and at Ayr was damaged.

Since 1945 St Ives has made great progress as a holiday centre, but the ever-increasing popularity of the motor car has brought many problems. A coach park and several large car parks have been constructed, and a comprehensive traffic scheme introduced to prevent the town's narrow streets becoming completely blocked by vehicles during the summer months.

In December 1949 a Mayoress's chain was presented to the Mayoress for that year, Mrs J. Payne. It comprises 49 rectangular panel-shaped links in 9 carat gold, each commemorating a Mayoress of the Borough, her name appearing on the front of the link, and the Mayor's on the reverse. The insignia of the chain consists of a main badge, with a reproduction of the Corporate seal in the centre, dated 1639. St Ives' first Lady Mayor, Mrs M. T. R. Pearce, was elected in 1953.

The town has expanded considerably of late years, large Council estates having been erected at Penbeagle and Carbis Bay, with flats for the elderly at Trewyn and Porthmeor, whilst there has been much private development also. In the Downlong area all the large pilchard curing cellars adjoining Porthmeor Beach have been replaced by blocks of flats, one of which, the Piazza, incorporates granite pillars of the old cellar in an interesting design.

St Ives suffered a major disaster in the early hours of July 24, 1970 when a fire which began in the Harbour Cafe on Wharf Road spread with fearful rapidity, fanned by a strong easterly wind. Leaping across Fore Street at the top of Court Cocking it ignited property adjoining Academy Steps, spreading to adjoining shops and the flats above. The firemen were handicapped in their efforts to halt the conflagration by lack of water pressure, whilst the tide was unfortunately out at the time, making it difficult to obtain a supply from the harbour. However, it was at last brought under control, though at one time the whole of this part of Downlong appeared doomed. Academy Terrace, in particular, had a fortunate escape. Altogether, four cafes, a large shop, four cottages and a garage were destroyed. Happily, there were no casualties, except the bull mastiff 'Tory' which had given first warning of the outbreak. The devastated area has since been reconstructed in a manner fully in keeping with its picturesque surroundings.

In the mid-19th century a semi-circular look-out enclosed by a granite wall was built in front of The Terrace, and named the Malakoff, from its supposed resemblance to the fortress of that name where an Anglo-French victory had been gained in the Crimean War. In 1972 this open space was laid out with seats and flower beds. The Malakoff Garden was opened on May 5 by Princess Anne—a gift to the people of St Ives and its visitors by the Round Table. A wheelwright's stone, from Newmill smithy, and a Hepworth bronze form distinctive features of the garden.

St Ives lost one of its best-known personalities in March 1974 with the death at the age of 73 of Abraham Curnow, its last town crier and loyal servant of the Borough for over half a century. 'Abr'am's' familiar voice and bell had won him a wide reputation, and people will never forget his friendliness, good nature and devoted service to the town.

St Ives' borough status ceased on April 1, 1974, the management of its affairs transferred to the new Penwith District Council at Penzance. So ended more than three and a quarter centuries of municipal independence. The loss has been keenly felt and deeply regretted by all sections of the community. From the wreck has been salvaged a Town Mayoralty and Council, but the power and the glory have departed, never, one fears, to return.

ABOVE: Life could be hard at St Ives in 1850 (RIC), and CENTRE: these railway workers deserved their break. (HF; EA); BELOW: Lelant station in broad gauge days, with the spur to Lelant wharves on the right. (RIC)

GREAT WESTERN RAILWAY.

"CONVERSION OF GAUGE."

This is the last Broad Gauge Train to travel over the Branch between

and

To the
Station Master

Traffic
Inspector

Station.

May 20th, 1892.

ABOVE: The trains brought tourists, and breathtaking vistas; the Carbis Valley viaduct was one vantage point (M; EA); CENTRE LEFT: Broad gauge engine *Magpie* at St Ives station (M; EA) and RIGHT: the end of the line for the old system (M). BELOW: St Ives station; Warren Gate left of the signal.

ABOVE : Building St Ives Board School in 1880—behind, Wheal Ayr engine
house; left, Eden House, home of the Treweeke family (M; EA); BELOW :
the town at that time. (M)

118

The terrible flood of 1894, ABOVE: rushing past the Wesleyan Chapel and
BELOW: leaving a battered home behind. (M; WTW)

LEFT: The Stennack beyond Rosewall Terrace, and Tregenna Place after the 1894 flood (WTW); ABOVE CENTRE: Island battery, dismantled March that year (M; EA) and BELOW: the Mayoral chain (TC; WT). CENTRE RIGHT: fun for the children of 1898 (M) and BELOW: the Duke of Cornwall's Light Infantry 2nd battalion on the Island in May 1899, during a march through Hayle, Lelant and onto Penzance (HF). RIGHT: Constable James Bennetts—the town's only protection in the late 19th century. (M)

TEMPLE'S & BECKETT'S
Animated Picture Company
WILL GIVE A SPECIAL

Living Picture
Entertainment

For SCHOOL CHILDREN for Advertisement.

A large number will be shown, including all the Latest

COMIC, LAUGHABLE, AND UP-TO-DATE PICTURES.

COME AND SEE THE
**COMICAL SPORTS, DONKEY RACE,
HAUNTED KITCHEN,
POLICEMAN'S DREAM, PILLOW FIGHT,
BULLER AT ALDERSHOT,
COMICAL HORSE, COMIC PICTURES OF
ALL KINDS, Also
RUSSO-JAPANESE WAR PICTURES.**

ADMISSION:
Front Seats, 2d.; Back Seats, 1d.
ADULTS.—Front Seats, 4d.; Back Seats, 2d.
Doors open at 5.15 p.m. Commence 5.30 p.m.

PRESENTS given to all Girls and Boys who
come to this Entertainment, such as Note and Picture Books,
Rings, Necklaces, sets of Playing Cards, etc., etc., etc.

Children in Front Seats have two presents, Back Seats
one present.

ABOVE: Taking a breather between airs at a town fete around the turn of
the century (HF); BELOW: local wheelwrights taking the air. (HF; EA)

122

ABOVE: A rare sylvan scene above the town (M) and BELOW: the harbour
idyll of nostalgic memory. (SSI)

LEFT: Charley Paynter introduces the 20th century in this 1900 picture—
he was Town Crier and town 'poet' (M); RIGHT: croquet (RIC; EA) and
BELOW: Porthminster Beach holidaymakers in the genteel atmosphere of
1904. (M)

ABOVE: A rare view of Porthgwidden and the Wood Pier from the Island
(PQ) and BELOW: looking the other way. (M)

Bluejackets Embarking at St Ives

ABOVE: The 1911 lull before the storm (RIC) when BELOW: blue jackets
embark from the harbour on the eve of World War I.

LEFT: The army leaves by train for the front, while essentials remain the same as RIGHT: Jim Pearce fetches water from St Ia's well at the foot of Porthmeor Hill. BELOW: better times with N. Tregurtha's and T. G. Wedge's rugby teams. (M)

Uncle Manuel of Love Lane carves his memories while INSET ABOVE:
Uncle Ephraim Perkin considers his and BELOW: Thomas Warren remem-
bers a century on his 100th birthday in 1963. (All M)

Man Friday Paynter would regale visitors with his tall tales of life before
the mast (M) while INSET: William Stevens attended to the realities of
of cleaning a pig. (SSI)

The Fire Brigade with ABOVE : their horse drawn engine St Ia and BELOW :
the motorised engine—the name's the same. (Both M)

RIGHT: The brigade had a busy time handling the Fore Street fire of 1970
(SB) while BELOW: a heavy duty hand was needed on Porthmeor Beach in
1967 to clear up the *Torrey Canyon* oil pollution (SB). LEFT: Abraham
Curnow, last St Ives Town Crier in full regalia and voice. (SB)

Before cars and congestion, a stroll through yesterday's town might start
LEFT: in the Stennack, at the old blacksmith's shop (SSI), passing RIGHT:
the old Sheaf of Wheat Inn, demolished for road widening. (SSI)

ABOVE: In Tregenna Place c1900 you could meet Garnet Carbines (left)
and Edward Webb, while BELOW: in 1896 the Passmore Edwards Institute
was yet to be built there. (M)

ABOVE: The old Manor House was where the post office now stands, and
BELOW: Dove Street led off Tregenna Place—the arched gateway marked
the entrance to Town Yard, once the almshouses. (M)

Looking up Skiden Hill. (SSI)

Along the Warren, within sound of the sea. (M)

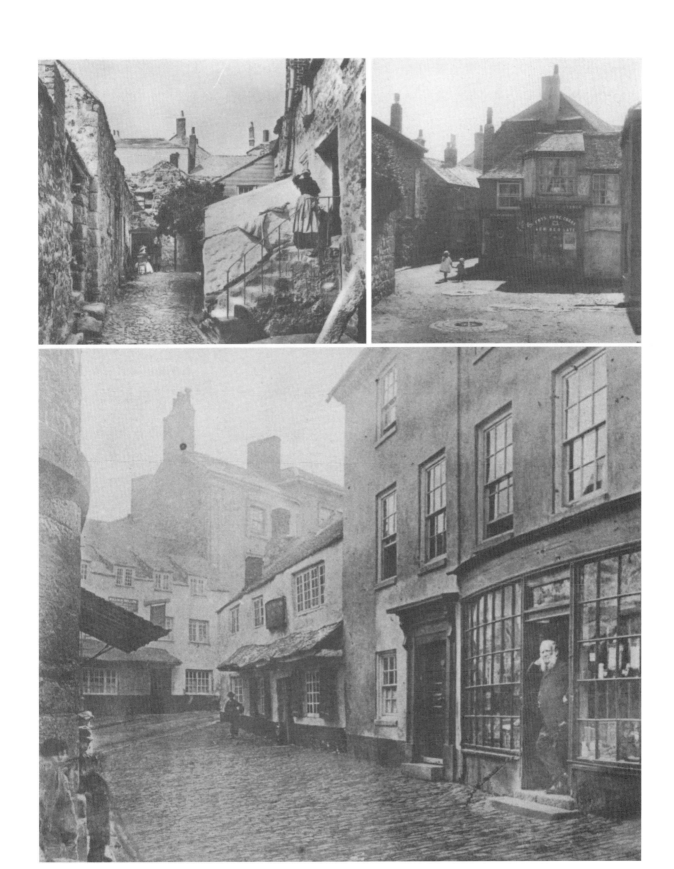

LEFT: Out of order—the vanished Pudding Bag Lane.
RIGHT: From St Andrew's Street to BELOW: the Market Place where the
Golden Lion (left) and George & Dragon (M) offered welcome refreshment.

ABOVE LEFT: High Street leads back from the Market Place, and BELOW: a lane and a street away, Barnoon Hill (RIC), leads to CENTRE: Academy Steps. (WT) RIGHT: Fore Street, where Goodman's grocery (now Brown's newsagency) was the second shop on the right when you left Market Place (M), and BELOW: The Cliffe (Fore Street). (LEC)

Up from Fore Street rises ABOVE LEFT: Virgin Street (1880) (M) and
RIGHT: nearby is The Digey. A few yards away BELOW LEFT: rises
Bunker's Hill (1904) (RIC) while not far off Fish Street leads away from
The Wharf. (M)

ABOVE: The Wharf itself, with the added attraction of Alfred Wallis' art studio (SSI) and BELOW: Back Road East to take us to The Island Square (SSI)

The steps, steep streets and simplicity that were and still are the essence of
St Ives.

Epilogue

The last edition of this book appeared in 1984, when Cyril Noall was preparing his fifth and final book in the series, which was published shortly after his death.

In arranging this third impression of his principal book on St Ives, we have agreed unanimously not to alter a word, or change a picture – though we are grateful to William Thomas, W. J. Watton and the British Library for new copies of original photographs, to improve some faded pages.

That there has been change to St Ives since 1977 and indeed 1984 is self-evident, but we have resisted the temptation to update Cyril's text.

The changes are not such as to diminish his work by their absence, for we believe he has captured the essence as well as the essential facts of St Ives' past and of its personality in these pages. To add our foreign facts would be to subtract from his native vision.

This is a full and proper record of a place bound by family and in friendship, through hardship and legend that, despite incomers, social change and economic pressures, remains essentially a close community, in its still cobbled streets, hemmed by its safe haven and sublime bay.

That is how Cyril saw it, how he recorded it, and how it should be presented. We commend *The Book of St Ives* in its original, unaltered state.

In doing so, we are all proud to have known Cyril, sad he cannot share this new publication of his most significant work, but confident that it will bring great pleasure and valued enlightenment to a new generation of St Iveans.

Greta Williams, Librarian
Brian Stevens, Curator
Clive Birch, Publisher   December 2000

Postscript 2011

Continuing demand for *The Book of St Ives* convinced us to see if it would be possible to produce a fourth edition. With the support of Clive Birch, Brian Stevens, William Thomas, The Town Council and the Friends of St Ives Library, and after great deliberation over format and costs, we are delighted to be able to present this new paperback edition. Apart from a new subtitle and foreword by Brian Stevens, and the 2000 edition Epilogue, the contents remain intact, as first published in 1977.

Christina Carson, Librarian
Jane Dews, Study Support Officer

Bibliography

Badcock, W., Historical Sketch of St Ives and District, *1896*.

Baker, Denys Val, Britain's Art Colony By The Sea, *1959*.

Barber, John T., Cousin Jack Afloat and Ashore, *1969*.

Blight, J. T., A Week at the Land's End, *1861*.

Bottrell, William, Traditions and Hearthside Stories of West Cornwall, 3 vols, *1870, 1873, 1880*.

Caple, S. Canynge, St Ives Scrap Book, *1961*.

Carew, Richard, Survey of Cornwall, *1602* (*1769 ed*).

Chope, R. Pearse (editor), Early Tours in Devon and Cornwall, *1918*.

Courtney, J. S., Guide to Penzance, *1845*.

Davies-Freme, Rev E. T., A Short Description of St Uny Lelant, *1947*.

Dines, H. G., The Metalliferous Mining Region of South West England, *1956*.

Doble, Canon G. H., Lananta, The Church and Parish of St Euny Lelant, *1939*.

—— St Euny, *nd*.

—— St Ives, Its Patron Saint and its Church, *1939*.

—— St Winwaloe, *1940*.

Dunstan, Mary, Trusty and Well-beloved: The Story of a Cornish Royalist (Francis Basset] *1956*.

F. C. H., Notes on the Church and Parish of Zennor, *1939*.

Garstin, Crosbie, Samuel Kelly, An Eighteenth Century Seaman, *1925*.

Gilbert, Davies, History of Cornwall, *1838*.

Gilbert, C. S., History of Cornwall, *1817*.

Gould, Rev S. Baring, Cornish Characters and Strange Events, *nd*.

Hain, Sir Edward, Prisoners of War in France, 1804-1814, *1914*.

Hencken, H. O'Neill, The Archaeology of Cornwall and Scilly, *1932*.

Henderson, Charles, The Cornish Church Guide, *1925*.

—— Cornish Essays, *1935*.

Hicks, John, History of St Ives (MS now lost), *1722*, quoted by C. S. Gilbert.

Hingeston, Francis, Poems, *1857*.

Hunt, Dr Robert, Popular Romances of the West of England, *1871*.

Lach-Szyrma, Rev W. S., A Short History of Penzance, St Michael's Mount, St Ives, and the Land's End District, *1878*.

Laity, R. P., St Ives in the 1800's, *1973*.

March, Edgar J., Sailing Drifters, *1952*.

Matheson, Greville E., Painters, Poets and Others in St Ives, *1936*.

—— Crooked Street: St Ives Streets in Rhyme.

Matthews, John Hobson, A History of the Parishes of St Ives, Lelant, Towednack and Zennor, *1892*.

Noall, Cyril, Beloved St Ives, *1957*.
—— The Story of St Ives Lifeboats, *1957*.
—— Cornish Lights and Shipwrecks, *1968*.
—— The Story of St Ives, *1970*.
—— Cornish Seines and Seiners, *1972*.
—— History of St Ives Fore Street Methodist Church, *1962*.
—— Tales of the Cornish Fishermen, *1970*.
—— Cornwall's Ports and Harbours, *1970*.
—— The Story of Cornwall's Lifeboats, *1970*.
—— Smuggling in Cornwall, *1971*.
—— St Nicholas' Chapel, St Ives, *1971*.
Noall, Cyril (and others), The History of St John's in the Fields, St Ives, *1972*.
Noall, Cyril, and Farr, Grahame, Wreck and Rescue Round the Cornish Coast, Vol. 2, *1965*.
Noall, Richard John, Little Feathers and Stray Fancies, *nd*
—— 'Sonnar Faist,' *1929*.
O. J. O. (L. R. Moir), St Ives Peep-Show, *nd*.
Paris, Dr J. A., Guide to the Mount's Bay, *1824*.
Paynter, Winifred, Old St Ives: The Reminiscences of William Paynter, *1927*.
Pearce, John, The Wesleys in Cornwall, *1964*.
Phillimore and Taylor, Cornish Parish Registers: Marriages, Vols ix and xiv, *1909*.
Polwhele, Rev R., Biographical Sketches in Cornwall, *1833*.
Pool, P. A. S., The Life and Progress of Henry Quick of Zennor, *1963*.
Praed, Winthrop Mackworth, Poems, *1864*.
—— Trash, *1833*.
Raymont, Mrs C. Morton, The Early Life of Robert Morton Nance, *1962*.
—— Memories of Old St Ives, *1958*.
Rogers, J. J., Notice of John Knill, *1871*.
Spray, Leonard, If You are Going to St Ives, *1952*.
Stephens, C. Taylor, The Chief of Barat-Anac, *1862*.
—— The Revival at St Ives, Cornwall, by the Rev William and Mrs Booth, *1862*.
Stone, J. Harris, England's Riviera, *nd*.
Warner, Rev Richard, A Tour Through Cornwall in the Autumn of 1808, *1809*.
Wigley, Joyce, and Dudley, Dorothy, Zennor, *nd*.
Williams, Col H. W., Some Reminiscences (1838-1918), *1918*.
St Ives, Cornwall, Tercentenary Celebrations (programme booklet with historical notes, etc), *1939*.
Nancledra Scrapbook (published by the Nancledra Women's Institute) *1951*.
The Borough of St Ives, 1639-1974 (commemorative booklet to mark the end of the Borough), *1974*.
St Ives Festival of Music and the Arts Programme Book, *1953*.

———

St Ives Parish Magazine (published under various titles from 1864, and possibly earlier.)
St Ives Weekly Summary, Visitors' List and Advertiser, *1889-1910*.
The Western Echo, *1899-1957*.
The St Ives Times, *1910*; merged with The Western Echo in *1957* to form The St Ives Times and Echo; The Royal Cornwall Gazette; The West Briton; The Cornish Telegraph;

The Cornishman; The Hayle Miscellany; The Cornish Magazine; Old Cornwall; Journal of the Royal Institution of Cornwall; The Journal of the Cornish Methodist Historical Association; The Journal of the Trevithick Society.

Index

146

147

Cyril Noall, specially painted in memoriam by JAD. Davies of St Ives;
the original hangs in St Ives Library, a copy in the Cyril Noall Room at
St Ives Museum.

KEY TO CAPTION LETTERS

SSI	Studio St Ives	HF	Harold Franklin	My	— Moody		
CRO	County Record Office	EA	Edward Ashton	JCD	J. C. Douglas		
WT	William Thomas	LEC	L. E. Cromley	PQ	Percy Quick		
TC	St Ives Town Council	TMB	T. M. Banfield	SB	S. Bennetts		
ETB	E. T. Berryman	RIC	Royal Institution of Cornwall	HJH	H. J. Healey		
M	St Ives Museum	PMGL	Penzance (Morrab Gardens) Library	DP	Daphne Pearson		
		WTW	William Trevorrow				

ENDPAPERS – FRONT: St Ives c1825. (CRO; WT)
BACK: St Ives Parish, from the 1877 Ordnance Survey. (By permission of
the British Library: Maps O.S.f.LX1:12)

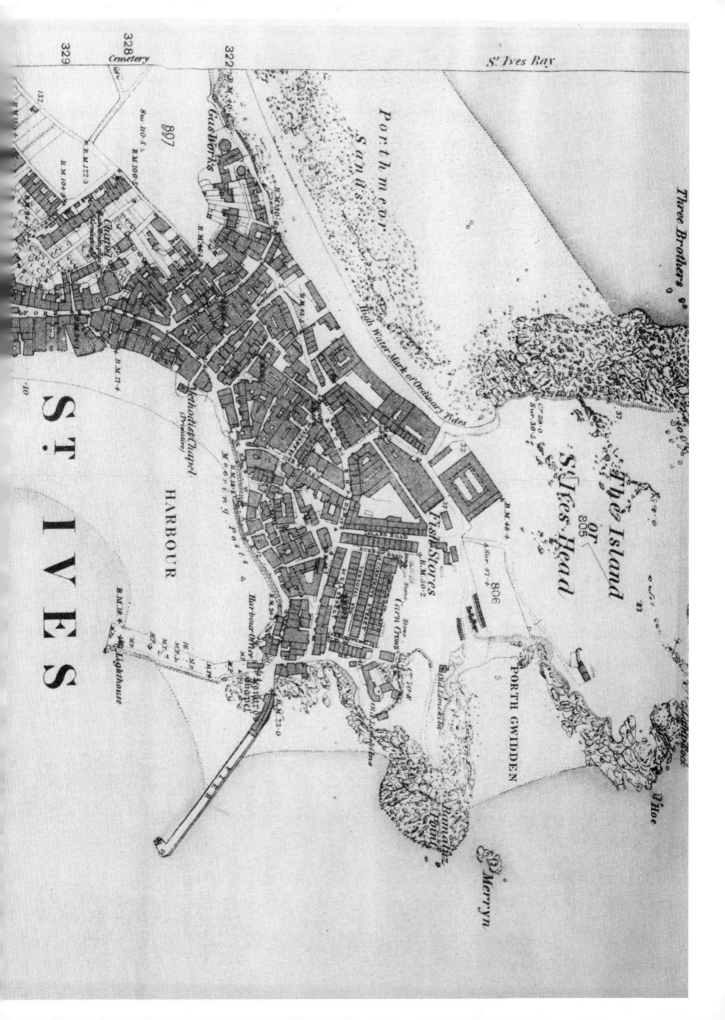